PENGUIN CLASSICS

ESSAYS IN IDLENESS
and HŌJŌKI

KAMO NO CHŌMEI (*c.* 1155–1216) was a prominent poet, essayist and musician associated with the court in Kyoto. At the age of fifty, personal setbacks and despair at the world led him to take the tonsure and retire to live in a hut beyond the city limits. Here, he wrote the three works for which he is now remembered – *Mumyōshō* (*Nameless Treatise*), *Hosshinshū* (*A Collection of Religious Awakenings*), and the famous *Hōjōki* (*Record of a Ten-foot-Square Hut*).

YOSHIDA KENKŌ (or Kaneyoshi) (*c.* 1283–*c.* 1352) was a poet, essayist and noted calligrapher. He took the tonsure probably in his late twenties, and underwent a period of rigorous monastic training, but for the most part continued to remain involved with life in the capital. The sole work for which he is now remembered, *Tsurezuregusa* (*Essays in Idleness*), a rich compendium of opinions and anecdotes, is counted among Japan's greatest classics.

MEREDITH MCKINNEY holds a Ph.D. in medieval Japanese literature from the Australian National University in Canberra, where she is currently a visiting fellow. She taught in Japan for twenty years, and now lives near Braidwood, New South Wales. Her other translations include *Ravine and Other Stories* by Furui Yoshikichi and, for Penguin Classics, *Kokoro* and *Kusamakura* by Natsume Sōseki and *The Pillow Book* by Sei Shōnagon.

PENGUIN CLASSICS

ESSAYS IN IDLENESS
and HŌJŌKI

KAMO NO CHŌMEI [illegible] was a prominent poet [illegible] musician who served at the court in Kyoto. At the age of fifty [illegible] setbacks and [illegible] him to take the tonsure and [illegible] the rest of his life. [illegible] for which he is now remembered [illegible] *Mumyōshō* [illegible] and the famous *Hōjōki* [illegible]

[illegible] for Yoshida [illegible] was a poet, essayist and calligrapher. He took the tonsure probably in his [illegible] and underwent a period of [illegible] but for the most part continued to remain involved with the world. The sole work for which he is now remembered, *Tsurezuregusa* [illegible], a rich compendium of opinions and anecdotes, is counted among Japan's greatest classics.

MEREDITH MCKINNEY [illegible] in medieval Japanese literature [illegible]

YOSHIDA KENKŌ AND
KAMO NO CHŌMEI

Essays in Idleness
and Hōjōki

Translated with an introduction and notes by
MEREDITH MCKINNEY

PENGUIN BOOKS

PENGUIN CLASSICS

Published by the Penguin Group
Penguin Books Ltd, 80 Strand, London WC2R ORL, England
Penguin Group (USA) Inc., 375 Hudson Street, New York, New York 10014, USA
Penguin Group (Canada), 90 Eglinton Avenue East, Suite 700, Toronto, Ontario, Canada M4P 2Y3
(a division of Pearson Penguin Canada Inc.)
Penguin Ireland, 25 St Stephen's Green, Dublin 2, Ireland (a division of Penguin Books Ltd)
Penguin Group (Australia), 707 Collins Street, Melbourne, Victoria 3008, Australia
(a division of Pearson Australia Group Pty Ltd)
Penguin Books India Pvt Ltd, 11 Community Centre, Panchsheel Park, New Delhi – 110 017, India
Penguin Group (NZ), 67 Apollo Drive, Rosedale, Auckland 0632, New Zealand
(a division of Pearson New Zealand Ltd)
Penguin Books (South Africa) (Pty) Ltd, Block D, Rosebank Office Park,
181 Jan Smuts Avenue, Parktown North, Gauteng 2193, South Africa

Penguin Books Ltd, Registered Offices: 80 Strand, London WC2R ORL, England

www.penguin.com

First published in Great Britain by Penguin Classics 2013

018

Set in 10.25/12.25pt Postscript Adobe Sabon
Typeset by Jouve (UK), Milton Keynes
Printed in Great Britain by Clays Ltd, Elcograf S.p.A

ISBN: 978–0–141–19210–9

www.greenpenguin.co.uk

Penguin Books is committed to a sustainable
future for our business, our readers and our planet.
This book is made from Forest Stewardship
Council™ certified paper.

Contents

Introduction

In a period roughly spanning the twelfth to fourteenth centuries in Japan, a vibrant and complex literary culture flowered from Buddhist teachings and practice. This book contains the two prose works that were the finest embodiments of that culture, and that still rank among Japan's great classics.

The men who wrote these works were tonsured monks, who had formally dedicated themselves to the practice of the Buddhist Way; they were not, however, attached to any monastery, and one of them (Yoshida Kenkō, 1283–1350) was actively involved in the social sphere of the capital (present-day Kyoto). In their different ways, these men belonged to a niche that gave them access to two contrasting worlds – the mundane and the religious – while allowing them to escape the more arduous demands of both. The freedom of their situation, along with its inherent tensions, was at the heart of the literature that they and others like them produced.

Buddhism in Japan had a long tradition of solitary practice for those who chose to distance themselves from the often intensely political world of the monasteries. The most impressive of these hermit ascetics were considered holy men, and accorded almost saintly status. Tales of their wisdom and the severity of their ascetic practice circulated among both monks and laity. They represented one extreme of the non-monastic Buddhist practitioner; the other was the figure of the 'lay monk' or *shami* (translated here as novice), who chose to take the tonsure as a means to retire from active engagement with the world, often in response to increasing age or to a setback in his career, but who frequently remained at home and continued to have limited dealings with the world. Such a gesture could be calculated or impulsive, sincere or merely formal.

Between the two extremes, and sometimes tending now towards one and now the other over the course of a life, was a wide range of men (and occasionally women) who went by a variety of titles, but generally fitted somewhere within the concept of the recluse monk, or *tonseisha*. These people, who inhabited a fluid realm in which they were largely their own master and could live as they wished, were the men who produced what is commonly called the literature of reclusion, whose two finest prose examples are *Hōjōki* and *Essays in Idleness* (*Tsurezuregusa*).

Kamo no Chōmei[1] (*c.*1155–1216) provides us in *Hōjōki* with the quintessential figure of the literary recluse. He has built for himself a tiny hut, exactly large enough to contain the essentials for life, in a remote place far from the distracting presence of others, where the peace and beauty of the natural surroundings are conducive to calm contemplation. His life is one of utmost simplicity. Prominent on the wall are two Buddhist images, with a sutra (a Buddhist scripture) placed on the altar before them, where he performs his religious devotions. The only other contents of the hut, apart from his bed of bracken, are a shelf that holds a few carefully chosen books (a religious tract, poetic anthologies and musical treatises) and two musical instruments. He divides his time, as the spirit takes him, between performing his devotions and reading the sutras and playing his instruments and reading or composing poetry. Despair at the sufferings of this world has led him to choose this life, but he is by his own admission a happy man.

The hermit-aesthete of *Hōjōki* is consciously following a venerable lineage reaching back to ancient China, some of whose finest poets belonged to this tradition of reclusion. In the Japan of the twelfth and thirteenth centuries, when Chōmei chose to live like this, his more immediate models were other Japanese non-monastic monks, of his time or earlier, who combined pursuit of a spiritual calling with an equal dedication to the arts, most particularly that of poetry. They are sometimes referred to as *suki no tonseisha*, hermit monks who united the ascetic and aesthetic modes, and for whom cultivation of an artistic sensibility was almost as important as one's spiritual practice. Although these men seldom lived quite the ideal life depicted in *Hōjōki*, the portrait we find there embodies the quintessential image of the *suki no tonseisha*. Sensitivity to the beauty of the natural world, and a simple and unaffected aesthetics, were essential aspects of the life of the cultured recluse, qualities which found later expression in the tea ceremony and the aesthetics of *wabi*, austere and artless beauty. Even the worldly and sociable Yoshida Kenkō of *Essays in Idleness*, who can be harsh about the delusions inherent in the life of the hermit-aesthete (see section 137), admires the moving simplicity of a lonely recluse's hut he visits, and disapproves when he finds evidence there of a lack of taste (section 11).

Chōmei and Kenkō, and the works they wrote, were in many ways so different that placing them within the one tradition might seem unjustifiable. It is a shock to move from Chōmei's tranquil seclusion in his little hut to the vigorous and shifting realm of Kenkō's engagement with the complexities of worldly life and how best to live it. More than a century separates the two works, a turbulent period in which much changed. Yet fundamental things unite them. Both these men, in their lives and in their writing, combined in an uneasy and fruitful union the two key elements of the literature of reclusion – religion (Buddhism) and the literary arts.

The Buddhist teaching of Impermanence (*mujō*) provided the crucial meeting point between the religious and literary realms. The mark of a person of feeling was *aware* – a poignant awareness of the transience of the phenomenal world, embodied alike in the changing seasons and in the shifting fortunes of human life. This crucial concept forms the locus where the stern Buddhist doctrine of Impermanence met and was softened by the aesthetics of deep responsiveness to the world typified in literary writing. Poetry, long a key marker of the cultured person, drew much of its power from this sense of *aware*, and both poet and audience could feel that they were savouring an essential Buddhist truth through a poem that evoked or sorrowed over ephemeral beauty.

Yet the cultivation of *aware* held a danger that the more strictly religious were quick to recognize – the Buddhist teaching on the impermanence of the phenomenal world pointed directly to the necessity for non-attachment, yet *aware* seemed often to be an end in itself, a way of binding one to this world through the moving experience of sighing over its passing beauty and delight. The recluse who relinquished worldly attachment only to divide his time between Buddhist devotion and artistic pursuit, as Chōmei did, was surely in peril of cancelling the one by the other. Against this accusation, the cultured recluse argued that depth of feeling and a strong awareness of the fleeting nature of the world could lead to a more profound understanding of the Buddhist Way, and that artistic pursuits such as poetry were a means of purifying and focusing the mind much like meditation.

Yet the relationship between aesthetic sensibility and Buddhism remained uneasy, as is evident in both *Hōjōki* and *Essays in Idleness*. Both authors were distinguished poets, for whom a life of refined sensibility was indispensable, yet both chose to dedicate themselves to Buddhism by formally taking the tonsure. The tensions of their double allegiance were expressed in differing ways – in Chōmei's case, in a sudden revulsion from the pleasure he took in the life of aesthetic reclusion; for Kenkō, in a disconcerting and largely unselfconscious veering between a fierce Buddhist ascetic philosophy and a worldly sense of the supreme importance of aesthetic taste and feeling. The *tonseisha*'s niche between the mundane and monastic worlds produced not only freedom but, frequently, a difficult tussle between ways of being that were at bottom hard to reconcile.

HŌJŌKI

Both Chōmei and Kenkō made the difficult choice to 'leave the home' (*shukke*, a Buddhist term meaning to relinquish one's place in the social world and take the tonsure) and devote themselves to the Buddhist Way against a background of severe political and social upheaval.

By the time of Chōmei's birth in around 1155, the stable world of the court, with the emperor as its symbolic head and the great family dynasty of the Fujiwaras providing the governance of the country, was rapidly breaking up. A century and a half earlier, imperial rule had become complicated by the institution of the powerful Retired Emperor's Office (*In no chō*), from which an emperor who had abdicated in favour of his often infant successor could effectively continue to wield influence over the course of his life, often meddling with the succession line and destabilizing court politics by forming allegiances among quarrelling factions.

Just such a combination of succession quarrels and internal power struggles within the Fujiwara family came to a head in 1155, precipitating the fateful decision by the parties involved to call on the help of two powerful military clans who had been slowly gaining strength in the provinces – the Genji (or Minamoto) and the Heike (or Taira) – to resolve the issue by force. The result of the complicated plots, attacks and counter-attacks that followed marked the beginning of the ascendancy of the military clans, who swiftly gained a foothold among the powerful at court, and fought it out with each other for supremacy in a struggle that eventually raged over much of the country. The immediate winner of the military clans' interference in court affairs was the head of the Heike clan, Taira no Kiyomori (1118–81). Kiyomori, who had helped the powerful retired emperor to victory, was rewarded with court rank, and quickly advanced through promotions to become effective ruler in 1167.

These political and military disruptions find no place in Chōmei's recital of the tragic events that he had witnessed over the course of his life. Perhaps tact stayed his hand, since the aftermath of these struggles was still being played out, or perhaps he chose for thematic purposes to concentrate his focus on natural rather than man-made disaster. Yet Kyoto was certainly affected by the pitched battles that raged around it during the years of the Genpei wars (as the clan fighting came to be known), and the famine that Chōmei depicts was a direct consequence of disruptions to supplies that would normally have been provided from more distant provinces to the drought-affected city. No doubt Chōmei was no more concerned than is any normal citizen with events that had no immediate effect on him, and he was perhaps largely unaware of the deeper implications in the day-to-day news of upheavals at court and battles that raged elsewhere in the country. But his lifetime was nevertheless a time of huge change, and its instability can be felt in the fervour with which he embraced the Buddhist teaching of Impermanence.

Although his final years were spent as a Buddhist monk, Chōmei was born into a family of Shinto priests. His father was the superintendent (*negi*) of Kamo Shrine, the great shrine that still stands today where Kyoto's two rivers meet. Its important imperial connections gave the shrine immense prestige, and Chōmei, as a child of only seven, had the proud experience of being given court rank. Such things were important to a career – though a power struggle already raged in the highest places, the imperial court was still the centre of the nation, and its ranks were a key to advancement among the capital's elite. But the trajectory of his life changed in his late teens when his father's illness and death caused the role of shrine superintendant to be transferred to another. *Hōjōki* also speaks of the loss of an inheritance through his grandmother, although the details of this are unclear. The result of these problems was that Chōmei was deprived of a future that had seemed assured, and found himself cast out upon the world as it was changing around him.

The details of Chōmei's career in the following decades remain unclear, but it is probable that he made his living through the prestigious skills of poetry and music that he had first acquired as a well-brought-up youth. He is recorded as playing an important part in the famous poetry circle known as Karin'en (Garden in the Poetic Woods), where prominent poets of the day from courtiers to recluse poets gathered to exchange and discuss poetry, and when he was twenty-seven he produced a volume of his own poems. The themes of lament and despair at the world evident in these poems are no doubt in part a reflection of the poetic style of the time, when many of the best poets were *tonseisha*, but it surely also reflects Chōmei's own experiences and sensibility.

Although it is for his other writing that Chōmei is remembered, he was an important though minor poet of his day, and when Retired Emperor Gotoba in 1201 gathered a group of compilers to work on his projected imperial anthology, the *Shinkokin Wakashū*, Chōmei was proud to be chosen among them. His diligence at the task prompted Gotoba to attempt to reward him by offering him the position of superintendent priest at a subsidiary shrine in the Kamo Shrine complex, a position that would re-establish Chōmei in something close to the role that fate had deprived him of in his youth. Unfortunately, the current incumbent at the Kamo Shrine objected to the appointment on the grounds that his own son had a higher claim. Gotoba attempted to make amends by offering Chōmei a similar position elsewhere, but Chōmei's wounds evidently went too deep. In an impulsive gesture that those around him considered mad, he simply disappeared, leaving it to rumour and a few parting poems to inform the world that he had taken the tonsure and 'thrown away the world'.

Chōmei was fifty when he made this momentous decision, already an old man by the standards of the day. His first impulse was to join the famous community of *tonseisha* at Ōhara, not far to the north of the capital. Here he later described himself as having passed 'five fruitless years'. Ōhara included a thriving group of recluse poets, whom he would have known, and it seems odd that the community was so little to his liking. But accounts suggest that Chōmei could be a prickly and somewhat difficult man, and perhaps he found distasteful the chaotic throng of hermits that by then inhabited what had begun as a remote and peaceful refuge from the world. Ōhara may well have proved to be almost as worldly as the world that he had so high-mindedly left behind. A diary account of the time describes him as looking gaunt and unhappy. Clearly Chōmei had still not found the inner peace he craved.

In around 1208, he had the great good fortune to be offered by an acquaintance at Ōhara the chance to abandon this unpalatable community. His friend had family connections with Hōkaiji Temple in Hino, to the south-east of the capital, and suggested that Chōmei build himself a retreat back in the hills on part of the temple land. Chōmei must have accepted with alacrity. *Hōjōki* takes up the tale of how he built for himself a tiny hut, ten feet square, hinged for easy dismantling and transport should he wish to move on, and later added a small veranda, and an awning beneath which he cooked and stored firewood. This is the *hōjō* (literally, ten-foot-square hut) of the title, and the deep delight in it that he records in *Hōjōki* has endeared him to readers down the centuries. Here he settled down to live at last the life he had yearned for, and it was probably here, in 1216, at the age of sixty-two, that he died.

The peace and happiness that Chōmei found at Hino flowered into the writing by which he is now remembered. During these seven or eight final years of life he produced three major works.[2] The first, *Mumyōshō* (*Nameless Treatise*), a two-volume collection of essays on poets and poetic matters, was completed around 1210. It distilled the teachings of his early poetry teacher Shun'e, and provides an invaluable reference for studies of the poetry of this important period. The other work besides *Hōjōki* that was written in these years is *Hosshinshū* (*A Collection of Religious Awakenings*), a much longer collection of tales of exemplary recluse monks, their lives and deaths, and their experience of Buddhist enlightenment.

These two very different works exemplify the dual worlds of the literary *tonseisha*. It is telling that, for all his urge for religious reclusion, the first thing that Chōmei chose to write in his ideal retreat was a treatise on poetry in which Buddhism is hardly present. The date of *Hosshinshū* is unknown, but it is probable that it was completed around 1214, several years after *Hōjōki* and not long before his death. The crucial final passage of *Hōjōki* certainly points to this likelihood. Here, in a volte-face that shocks the reader lulled by his depiction of the pleasures of his present life, Chōmei turns on himself with a fierce accusation: 'You fled the world to live among forest and mountain in order to discipline the mind and practise the Buddhist Way. But though you have all the trappings of a holy man, your heart is corrupt.' Attachment to his hut and the happy life he leads there have perverted the purity of his original vow to turn his back on the impermanent and illusory world and seek salvation.

Henceforth, it seems, he will dedicate himself to his religious devotions, and study, not the poets but men who lived and died well as enlightened Buddhists.

Hōjōki thus embodies the tension inherent in the life of the aesthete recluse. Readers and scholars down the centuries have struggled to reconcile the ending with all that leads up to it, unwilling to allow a work so coherently constructed to betray itself on its final page. In fact, this last short section works as an admonitory shock to the reader, who has allowed him- or herself to be led astray precisely as has Chōmei, relishing with him his pleasure in his hut instead of holding in mind the teaching of the work's earlier sections, that all is impermanent and all attachment folly. Chōmei surely knew what he was about when he added this final, deeply heartfelt, coda. We stand accused by it as he does, although later, less austerely devout ages have retreated from the challenge to join him in his penitent commitment to Buddhist salvation.

Hōjōki is tightly structured in a progression from elegant prologue stating the theme of impermanence, through a series of vivid vignettes that hammer home the message by depicting the numerous calamities that Chōmei has witnessed, followed by a brief general discussion of the inconstancies of life, which leads to his own story of despair at the world and retreat from it to seek salvation. Although it echoes the structure of a sermon, his genius is to not simply preach but to draw us in by experiencing with him, first, the tragic events he has witnessed that point the message, then the answer he has found for himself, which seems for a while to provide what is finally revealed as a false solution. The structure hinges on the figure of the house, referred to in the opening passage as a 'brief dwelling' (*kari no yadori*), in a phrase that would instantly alert readers of the time to its poetic and Buddhist symbology, the impermanent 'passing shelter' of our fleshly existence during our brief life on earth.

Chōmei's summary of the progress of his own life, from the fine mansion of his youth through a series of diminishing houses to the tiny 'brief dwelling' of his few final years, traces a trajectory that mirrors his slow realization of the truth of impermanence. The hut he builds is in itself a clear statement of his Buddhist commitment. The original *hōjō* was the ten-foot-square hut traditionally believed to be the home of the early lay Buddhist saint Vimilakīrti, described in the *Vimilakīrti Nirdesa Sutra*. *Hōjōki*'s famous opening lines are a close echo of the words of this sutra,[3] which is an implied presence behind the work and its themes, and in the final section Chōmei explicitly condemns himself for failing to live up to the wisdom of this man whom he hoped to emulate through the model of his dwelling.

Hōjōki is self-consciously part of a long tradition of writings on the serene life of the hermit in his hut. The depth and complexity of this tradition, of which the average Western reader can scarcely be aware, adds rich texture to this work. Readers of his time would have savoured the resonances with past tradition, both literary and Buddhist, that infuse the work, and at the same time registered its freshness. Others before him in both China and Japan had written similar prose pieces in praise of the simple dwellings to which they retired,[4] for the most part charming and largely straightforward personal essays. But *Hōjōki* is much more than this: a work that aims to rise above the merely personal and anecdotal both through its larger religious themes and through the elegance of its structure and its prose.

From the opening section, the reader is aware of the theme of the dwelling, whose literal and religious imagery binds the work together. The disasters that Chōmei so vividly describes are all unobtrusively presented through the fate of houses, so that the account of his tiny hut, when it finally arrives, is experienced as much more than the simple description of happy retirement that it might otherwise seem. The very term for the act of leaving the world to become a monk, 'leaving the house' or home, here takes on an added resonance – the 'house' of the expression is no longer a mere metaphor for the household with all the worldly attachments and obligations that it implies, but the physical dwelling, whose ephemerality is now felt as a metaphor for the ephemeral nature of existence itself. So the theme of dwellings and their impermanence naturally points to 'leaving the house' and embracing the Buddhist Way, and the religious truth that the first half of the work preaches finds its natural expression in the hermit's hut, the recluse's 'passing shelter' whose serenity aids him in his preparation for his end. As that end approaches with the end of *Hōjōki* itself, even this hut is cast away at the realization of the necessity of non-attachment, the lesson that lies behind the sermon preached by this work.

This thematic elegance is echoed by the elegance of *Hōjōki*'s prose. Chinese, long the language of Buddhism and of formal written expression in Japan, had by Chōmei's day begun to be integrated into written native Japanese. Chōmei drew on his educated ear for Chinese literary rhythms to infuse the prose of *Hōjōki* with a poetically heightened intensity. In its most sonorous sections, such as the opening paragraphs, the language follows not only the construction of poetic Chinese writing, where phrases echo and balance against each other within the sentence, but sometimes its inverted word order, and it would have rung with the authority of a Buddhist sermon for a contemporary audience. Elsewhere, where he describes the catastrophes he has witnessed, the tone shifts to one of terse, almost colloquial directness. Throughout this work Chōmei was at pains to infuse his language with all the force and poetry that the written styles of the day afforded, and the reader is carried forward as much by the rhetorical power of the prose as by the words themselves.

ESSAYS IN IDLENESS

Hōjōki is written in the form of a personal memoir, but its tight focus and close thematic patterning in fact exclude much that we might expect to find in such a work. Not only the violent political upheavals of the day and their accompanying warfare and disruption, but the main events of Chōmei's own life and indeed any real sense of the man himself are missing from this account. *Hōjōki* presents an almost abstract portrait, the figure in outline of a man who has beheld and understood the transient nature of this world of suffering, and turned from it to seek solace and salvation in religion and the ideal life of the *tonseisha* in his hut. With Yoshida Kenkō's *Essays in Idleness* (*Tsurezure-gusa*), however, we immediately find ourselves in the realm of the personal. Kenkō too was a *tonseisha*, and he shared Chōmei's double devotion to poetry and religion, but where Chōmei was finally brought to a crisis of confrontation with the inherent contradictions between the aesthetic and ascetic modes, Kenkō, both in his writing and in his life, was happy to let contradictions and complexities stand.

Kenkō was born in around 1283, into a world that had come to its own awkward accommodations with a complex reality. The fierce clashes that Chōmei had witnessed a little over a hundred years earlier had irrevocably shifted power from the old imperial court system based in Kyoto to a new clan warrior shogunate that ruled from the provincial stronghold of Kamakura, near present-day Tokyo. Kyoto, where Kenkō was born and lived, remained the nominal capital, with a still-functioning court and reigning emperor, but these trappings of power were largely empty, and the Kamakura government maintained a base in Kyoto through which it controlled local affairs. Nevertheless, the emperor retained immense symbolic importance, and disputes over imperial succession could be as tangled and sometimes as fraught as they were in Chōmei's time.

These complications had led to an arrangement, begun in 1287, when Kenkō was a child, whereby two alternative imperial lines took turns to provide the emperor of the day. This problematic system on the whole functioned surprisingly well until 1321, when the ambitious Emperor Godaigo decided to assert his ancient imperial prerogative and rule in fact as well as symbolically. In 1321 he abolished the institution of retired emperor, where real imperial power had lain for so long, and then set about plotting the more difficult task of overthrowing the Kamakura government. Details of the planned *coup d'état* leaked out, and those involved were exiled, although Godaigo was spared punishment. Another attempt in 1331 saw him exiled himself. The turmoil did not end, however. Godaigo escaped from exile two years later, returned to brief victory, and then, through a complex series of betrayals and shifting alliances, both he and the Kamakura government itself were defeated by another military family, the Ashikagas, who proceeded to establish their new rule back in Kyoto replete with alternative emperor, while Godaigo set up a rival court in the hills that was to continue battling the central government for nearly half a century.

It is probable that *Essays in Idleness* was completed not long before Godaigo's defeat and exile in 1331, and a frequently accepted opinion dates it from 1329 or 1330 to 1331. However, no manuscript from Kenkō's time survives, and there are few hints in the work that help to date it. Opinions differ as to when it was begun, with some scholars favouring the view, based on conceptual and expressive discrepancies, that the first thirty-two sections were written much earlier, perhaps around 1319. It seems likely, in fact, that it was written over time rather than at a single date, and possible that Kenkō added further touches after 1331.

Like Chōmei, though perhaps for different reasons, Kenkō chose to avoid direct mention of the political upheavals and occasional outright warfare of his day, although they form the backdrop to much that he describes, and would have touched him closely at times. He frequently laments the past, when the courtly culture that he loved was in its heyday and unsullied by the rougher ways of the contemporary world, but he was a pragmatic man. Where Chōmei was prone to gloom and to impulsive reactions that led him to flee the mundane world and bury himself ever deeper in the hills, Kenkō, for all his admonitions to do likewise, was in fact far too intrigued by the world to turn his back on it. The contradictions that drove Chōmei to despair and self-accusation sit happily together in Kenkō's writing, and in his life. His times demanded adaptability to an often inconsistent and multi-layered world, and he was a man well suited to his times.

Like Chōmei, Kenkō was born into a Kyoto family of hereditary Shinto priests, although the tradition had died out in his grandfather's day. In his youth he was a retainer to the important aristocratic Horikawa family, which gave him court rank and automatically established him in an alliance with one of the two alternative imperial lines, that to which Emperor Godaigo later belonged. In the normal course of things, he could have expected to stay in the lower echelons of the court, playing its petty politics and jostling for rank in a system that had by now lost all vestige of its original meaning and purpose. It is unclear when and why he decided to take the tonsure, although his poetry suggests that it was a difficult decision over which he wavered for some time. He is given the title of monk (*gobō*) in a record of a land purchase in 1313, when he would have been around thirty, and from this it is generally assumed that he formally took the tonsure some time in his late twenties.

Kenkō's movements beyond this point are unclear, although it is known that he settled in a house (probably rather more than a hut, to judge from his ideas on what was desirable in a dwelling; see, for instance, section 10) at Ono, on the edge of the city limits. At some point in his early years he spent time undergoing rigorous Buddhist training at Yokawa, part of the great temple complex on Mount Hiei, and many passages in *Essays in Idleness* make it clear that he remained a staunch, at times vehement, believer in the necessity of throwing all away and embracing the Buddhist Way. It is equally clear, however, that his own life generally bore little resemblance to Chōmei's ideal hermit in his hut. He was skilled in poetry, still the mark of the cultured man – although like Chōmei he remained below the first rank of poets of his day – and for much of his life was closely associated with the conservative Nijō school of poetry in Kyoto. This seems to have given him not only a secure place in the cultural circles of the time, but also an income, through poetry correction and copying (he was a noted calligrapher as well). His worldly familiarity extended well beyond the realm of the arts, however. References in *Essays in Idleness* (see, for instance, sections 34 and 119) show that he made one or more visits east to Kamakura, the military government stronghold of the day, and he was on easy terms with both the refined world of the Kyoto court and the warrior classes who were increasingly invading life in the old capital. Although when the mood took him he could be a fierce advocate of the world-loathing that was the current flavour of more extreme Buddhist belief at the time, Kenkō remained essentially a man of the world, keen to observe, participate in and record it in all its aspects.

Essays in Idleness reflects this open, fluid approach to life that was so in tune with the changeable times. It shifts with sometimes breathtaking ease between religious diatribe and cheerful personal anecdote, pedantic stipulations on correct court procedure and musings on how to gamble, become rich or drink with friends. There are common themes that reappear throughout the work – a concern with propriety is one (many parts of *Essays in Idleness* can be read almost as a gentleman's manual), together with a focus on past precedent that can at times seem ridiculously fussy and hidebound. Though he was often willing to put aside his prejudice against the boorish military classes who flooded the capital, his heart remained with the old high culture of Japan's past, still represented by the court and its traditions, and he was intent on shoring up what he could of this rapidly fading world and its sensibility.

The interest in aesthetics that is another strong thread running through this work also surely springs in part from this desire to stem the tide of coarseness and vulgarity that came with military rule and the waning of courtly values. *Aware* – the poignant sense of the brevity of things – is a key concept for Kenkō, expounded most famously in the opening paragraphs of section 137. He is surprised to discover this sense of pathos even in the 'alarming-looking ruffian' of section 142, but it is above all the sensitivity to beauty and refinement of the old culture that embodies all things good for Kenkō. His ideal man or woman is one who displays an innate understanding of this sensibility, and many of his anecdotes serve to record instances of such people.

For all its underlying continuities, however, it is in the sheer wealth of often conflicting opinions, tales, musings and harangues that the rich pleasures of *Essays in Idleness* truly lie. Where *Hōjōki* strives to maintain a tight thematic focus and development that keeps the portrait of its writer largely one-dimensional, *Essays in Idleness* sprawls across the gamut of thought and experience of a complicated and cheerfully inconsistent man. It is written with apparent artlessness in a string of sections of greatly varying length, rather like an occasional journal into which all kinds of passing thoughts are jotted. Continuities between sections can certainly be found, but it is the nature of *Essays in Idleness* to constantly surprise.

The effect of spontaneity is established by the opening lines, which claim for the following work the humble status of mere random jottings set down to while away the tedious hours. This disclaimer need not be taken at face value. It follows a tradition of self-deprecatingly shrugging off any claims for a work that the author is nevertheless happy to leave at the public's disposal, and Kenkō's dismissal of his act of writing as 'folly' should in no way be seen as the equivalent of Chōmei's fierce self-condemnation at the end of *Hōjōki*. Nevertheless, he clearly means to warn a potential reader that what follows is by nature haphazard and incoherent, and to excuse himself in advance for its erratic nature.

In fact, it is unlikely that a reader coming to the work would have been either surprised or disappointed by its fragmentary structure. Japanese literature had long favoured the disconnected, the series of small pieces at best only tangentially related. In earlier writing, this structure could be found in the contextualizing tales that tended to accompany poems, most famously in the work known as *The Tales of Ise* (*Ise monogatari*, late ninth or early tenth century). At their best, such works were more than simple collections. The reader's pleasure lay partly in the subtle weave of discontinuities and cross-echoes between the independent *dan* (sections), and the apparently spontaneous swervings and shifts could be savoured precisely for their element of surprise.

The supreme work of this kind was *The Pillow Book* (early eleventh century), a compendium of apparently random lists, anecdotes, opinions and musings by a gentlewoman at the empress's court, Sei Shōnagon (?966–?1017), which is one of the great classics of Japanese literature. Kenkō makes several references to the work (sections 1, 19, 138), and it is evident that he had its model in mind when he wrote his *Essays*, some sections of which echo her writing. But Kenkō was a very different person living in a very different age, for all his yearning back to the heights of Japanese culture and sensibility that *The Pillow Book* embodied. The structure and style of *The Pillow Book* clearly influenced Kenkō as he took up his brush to write, but what he produced bore only a formal resemblance to the earlier work.

Essays in Idleness is in fact as eclectic in its mix of influences and styles as in its heterogeneous content. The court manual, with its prescriptive detailing of ritual and procedure, is a likely presence behind some of the sections (e.g. 66 or 100). Pieces in a more lyrical mode (such as sections 32 or 104) hark back in style and sensibility to the earlier Heian literature of women's diaries and tales such as the great *Tale of Genji* (*Genji Monogatari*, 1004–?12), which evoke a lost world of high culture that Kenkō at times strove to emulate.[5] Kenkō could also draw on a more recent tradition of collections of short anecdotes on various topics, Kamo no Chōmei's *Mumyōshō* (*Nameless Treatise*) among them. But perhaps the most pervasive presence behind *Essays in Idleness*, both in content and in style, is that of Buddhist texts. These ranged from vernacular sermons and evangelical writings to the popular moral tales (*setsuwa*) that circulated among the laity. When Kenkō's mind turns to religious matters, the tone often grows stern. The language tends to shift towards the heavily Chinese-inflected Japanese that had continued to evolve from the influence of Buddhist writing since Chōmei's day, while the writing style is typified by pithy and didactic statement – a very different effect from the loose, elegant, descriptive sentences of Kenkō's more lyrical moments.

As is common in much of classical Japanese literature, the language of *Essays in Idleness* constantly weaves in quotations and allusions to past works. Familiarity with the poetry of the past, both Japanese and to a lesser extent Chinese, was the mark of any educated man (it was less common for educated women to have much learning in Chinese), and the Confucian classics are a strong presence in much of Kenkō's thinking and writing. A section such as section 7, with its poetic musing on the stock theme of ephemerality, builds its effects partly through the resonance of quotations and glancing references to Japanese poetry and Chinese classics, which add a depth and persuasiveness that readers of the time would have registered with considerable pleasure. Much scholarship has been devoted to identifying the often fleeting literary allusions that pervade

Essays in Idleness and produce a fineness of texture that modern readers can scarcely appreciate. Of necessity, only the more important references are noted in this translation.

In section 19, suddenly conscious that much of what he has just been writing merely echoes what can be found in earlier literature, Kenkō justifies himself by remarking that 'things thought but left unsaid only fester inside you. So I let my brush run on like this for my own foolish solace; these pages deserve to be torn up and discarded, after all, and are not something others will ever see.' For all that this smacks of the kind of false humility we can also detect in the preface, and is belied by the tone of direct address that he adopts elsewhere, it seems reasonable to assume that Kenkō was not writing with a specific readership in mind. Much of his advice was perhaps the kind of thing he would have wished to say to a well-bred young man attempting to make his way in the complex world of contemporary life in the capital, where (as Kenkō at least still believed) the niceties of the old courtly sensibility and way of life should be maintained and cultivated wherever possible, but the pragmatic man also needed to know his way around the brasher and more rough-and-tumble world of the warrior class that now held effective power. But just as *Essays in Idleness* resists all attempts to pin it down to a single form, style or theme, so we must in the end accept Kenkō's word that he was writing, not for any identifiable audience, but ultimately to say what was in his mind simply for the sake of saying it, as any keeper of a private journal will do. The fact that he seems at times aware of an audience, and that he apparently left the work to be found after his death, only adds another layer of inconsistency to the many that the work contains.

NOTES

1. *Kamo no Chōmei*: This is the name by which he is conventionally known. It is arguable that he would have preferred to be remembered by his Buddhist name, Ren'in, which is the name he appended to the end of *Hōjōki*.

2. *three major works*: Doubts remain about the authorship of *Hosshinshū*, but it is generally agreed that it is most probably by Kamo no Chōmei.
3. *the words of this sutra*: 'This body is like a mass of foam that is intangible. It is like a bubble that does not last long.' (Translation by Charles Luk, *Vimalakirti Nirdesa Sutra*, Berkeley: Shambhala Publications, 1972.)
4. *Others before him . . . to which they retired*: Chief among them are the Chinese poet Bai Juyi and retired Japanese official and littérateur Yoshishige no Yasutane (*Chiteiki*, *Record of the Pond Pavillion*, 982). There is no direct evidence that Chōmei had read the first work, although it is likely that he did, but *Hōjōki* has conscious echoes of the second.
5. *a lost world of high culture . . . strove to emulate*: It is interesting to note the almost complete absence of poetry in *Essays in Idleness*, despite the importance of poetry both in Kenkō's professional life and in the literary tradition he so valued. Prose writing in Japan could, and frequently did, include poetry, but both Kenkō and Chōmei apparently chose to keep their prose largely free of poems.

Further Reading

PRIMARY TEXTS

Leys, Simon (Translation and Introduction). *The Analects of Confucius*. New York: W. W. Norton, 1997.

McKinney, Meredith (Translation and Introduction). *The Pillow Book*. London: Penguin Classics, 2006.

Thurman, Robert A. F. (Translation and Introduction). *Vimalakirti Nirdesa Sutra*. University Park: Pennsylvania State University Press, 1976.

Tyler, Royall (Translation and Introduction). *The Tale of the Heike*. New York: Viking Penguin, 2012.

Watson, Burton (Translations and Introduction). *Four Huts: Asian Writings on the Simple Life*. Boston: Shambhala Publications, 1994.

SECONDARY TEXTS

Carter, Steven D. *Literary Patronage in Late Medieval Japan*. Ann Arbor: University of Michigan, Center for Japanese Studies, 1993.

Chance, Linda H. *Formless in Form*. Stanford: Stanford University Press, 1997.

Hare, Thomas. 'Reading Kamo no Chōmei'. *Harvard Journal of Asiatic Studies* 49, no. 1 (June 1989): 173–228.

LaFleur, William R. *The Karma of Words: Buddhism and the Literary Arts in Medieval Japan*. Berkeley: University of California Press, 1983.

Marra, Michele. *The Aesthetics of Discontent: Politics and Reclusion in Medieval Japanese Literature.* Honolulu: University of Hawaii Press, 1991.

Marra, Michele. *Representations of Power: The Literary Politics of Medieval Japan.* Honolulu: University of Hawaii Press, 1993.

Marra, Michele. 'Semi-Recluses (*tonseisha*) and Impermanence (*mujō*): Kamo no Chōmei and Urabe Kenkō'. *Japanese Journal of Religious Studies* vol. 11, no. 4 (December 1984): 313–50.

Mezaki, Tokue. 'Aesthete-Recluses during the Transition from Ancient to Medieval Japan'. In *Principles of Classical Japanese Literature*, ed. Earl Miner. Princeton: Princeton University Press, 1985.

Pandey, Rajyashree. *Writing and Renunciation in Medieval Japan: The Works of the Poet-Priest Kamo no Chōmei.* Ann Arbor: University of Michigan, Center for Japanese Studies, 1993.

Washburn, Dennis C. 'The Burden of the Future: Asserting the Literary Self in *Hōjōki*'. In *The Dilemma of the Modern in Japanese Fiction.* New Haven: Yale University Press, 1995.

Note on the Translation

Several variants of the *Hōjōki* text, displaying minor textual differences, have come down to us. This translation is from the 1244 Daifukukōji-bon. There is little doubt that this is the earliest text, and a postscript states that it is in the hand of Kamo no Chōmei himself. I have based my translation on the text as found in the *Shin Nihon Bungaku Taikei* edition.

The text of *Tsurezuregusa* presents a more complex history. The earliest transcription we have, known as Shōtetsu-bon (dated 1431), has numerous textual problems and cannot be thought to preserve unchanged the original form of the work. The present translation is based on the Karasumaru-bon (dated 1613), which is the textual form in which *Tsurezuregusa* has long been read.[1] No textual line is without its problems, however, and in this translation I choose from among the several other variants available on the few occasions where the text as preserved in the Karasumaru-bon seems problematic. All such textual choices are noted.

Names and titles present frequent translation problems, particularly in *Essays in Idleness*, which follows the common practice of referring to people by title rather than name, and frequently by the kind of associative epithet that was the fashion at the time. I have attempted to clarify such places, either with a note or occasionally by substituting the name, where known.

Religious titles present a more difficult problem. The complexity of the religious world of medieval Japan defies direct translation, and readers should be aware that religious titles and other terms that appear in the translation bear little relation to the Western religious tradition. Clerical ranks were complex, and titles such as *sōzu* or *hōin* have no equivalent in English. For these two titles, I substitute the title 'abbot', which should be taken to broadly refer to a high-ranking cleric. Lesser ranks are usually simply given the name 'priest'. Besides titles relating to monastic ranking, there are also numerous more general terms, such as *hōshi* (a general term for one who has taken the tonsure, translated here as 'monk')[2] and *nyūdō* (a lay monk or novice who may or may not continue to live in the family home), which can only be very approximately conveyed in translation.

I have chosen to retain the title *Hōjōki* for Kamo no Chōmei's work, which has variously been translated as 'An Account of My Hermitage'[3] and 'Record of the Ten-Foot-Square Hut'.[4] For Yoshida Kenkō's *Tsurezuregusa* (a more difficult name for the English speaker to retain), the title chosen by its early translator G. B. Samson[5] in 1911 and later used by Donald Keene for his 1967 translation[6] cannot be surpassed for both euphony and precision. *Tsurezure*, the opening word of the work itself, has the primary meaning of tedious time spent in idleness, while *gusa* (literally 'grass' or 'herbs') was a term conventionally used for personal and informal writings, much like the earlier meaning of the word 'essay'.[7]

NOTES

1. *the textual form . . . has long been read*: The Shōtetsu-bon text was discovered only in 1932, and although several modern editions of *Tsurezuregusa* are based on it, the Karasumaru-bon version is still the most widely read. I have referred to the text as found in the Shōgakukan edition (*Nihon Koten Bungaku Taikei*, 1995).
2. *'monk'*: It should be noted that a *hōshi*, whether of the monastic or lay tradition, could perform priestly functions such as sutra-saying for the laity (see *Essays in Idleness*, section 188 for a humorous description of such a man).
3. *An Account of My Hermitage*: Helen Craig McCullough, *Classical Japanese Prose: An Anthology*, Stanford: Stanford University Press, 1990.

4. *Record of the Ten-Foot-Square Hut*: Burton Watson, *Four Huts: Asian Writings on the Simple Life*, Boston: Shambhala Publications, 1994.
5. *G. B. Samson*: *Kenkō: Essays in Idleness*, London: Wordsworth Classics of World Literature, 1998.
6. *by Donald Keene for his 1967 translation*: *Essays in Idleness: The* Tsurezuregusa *of Kenkō*, New York: Columbia University Press, 1967.
7. *'essay'*: The work is traditionally divided into numbered sections. I have retained this numbering for ease of reference, although the early manuscripts do not include numbers, allowing the sections a more fluid relation to each other.

Essays in Idleness
and Hōjōki

HŌJŌKI

On flows the river ceaselessly, nor does its water ever stay the same. The bubbles that float upon its pools now disappear, now form anew, but never endure long. And so it is with people in this world, and with their dwellings.

In our dazzling capital the houses of high and low crowd the streets, a jostling throng of roof and tile, and have done so down the generations – yet ask if this is truly so and you discover that almost no house has been there from of old. Some burned down last year and this year were rebuilt. Others were once grand mansions, gone to ruin, where now small houses stand.

And it is the same with those that live in them. The places remain, as full of people as ever, but of those one saw there once now only one or two in twenty or thirty still survive. Death in the morning, at evening another birth – this is the way of things, no different from the bubbles on the stream.

Where do they come from, these newborn? Where do the dead go? I do not know. Nor do I know why our hearts should fret over these brief dwellings, or our eyes find such delight in them. An owner and his home vie in their impermanence, as the vanishing dew upon the morning glory. The dew may disappear while the flower remains – yet it lives on only to fade with the morning sun. Or perhaps the flower wilts while the dew still lies – but though it stays, it too will be gone before the evening.

Over the more than forty rounds of seasons since I first grew conscious of the world about me, I have seen many extraordinary things.

It would have been the twenty-eighth day in the fourth month of the third year of Angen.[1] The wind was fierce and the night tumultuous, and at the Hour of the Dog[2] a fire broke out in the capital's south-east, and spread to the north-west. Eventually the Shujaku Gate, the Hall of State, the University Hall and the Civil Affairs Bureau[3] all caught fire, and in a single night were reduced to ashes.

It was said the fire started in Higuchi Tominokōji, and began in a lodging house where some dancers were staying. The flames spread hither and yon on the fickle wind, fanning out wide over the city. Houses beyond were choked with smoke, while from those nearby, flames spouted and sparks rained down. Clouds of ash poured up into the sky, lit red by the fire beneath, and in the midst of all this blazing scarlet the ragged flames leaped whole blocks at a time, flying unresisting on the wind. For those caught up in the blaze, it must have seemed a nightmare. Some fell, choked with smoke; others were blinded by the flames and quickly perished. Where others managed to escape with their life, they left behind them all their worldly goods. All those countless treasures were turned to dust and ashes. How much was lost, all told?

In this fire sixteen noble houses alone were destroyed, not to mention the countless others. It is said that fully one-third of the capital was lost. Scores of men and women died, and who knows how many horses and oxen besides?

All human undertaking is folly, but it is most particularly futile to spend your wealth and trouble your peace of mind by building a house in the perilous capital.

Again, in the fourth month of the fourth year of Jishō[4] a great whirlwind sprang up in the Nakamikado Kyōgoku area, and swept down through the city to around Rokujō.[5]

Over three or four blocks, every single house, large or small, in the path of the swirling wind was destroyed. Some were utterly flattened, while only the pillars and beams of others remained. The wind tore up gates[6] and brought them down four or five blocks away. It blew away fences, making houses one with their neighbours. Needless to say, every last belonging inside the houses flew into the air, while cypress bark thatch and shingles[7] swirled in the gale like winter leaves. The wind raised such a spiralling smoke of dust that the eye was quite blinded, and the dreadful roar drowned out all speech. The karmic wind[8] of hell itself would be such as this, it seemed. Not only houses were damaged – countless people were hurt or maimed in trying to repair them. At length the wind moved off south-south-west, causing grief to many.

Whirlwinds are quite common, but do they ever blow like this? This was no ordinary wind, and all wondered whether it was not some portent from on high.

Also in the sixth month of the fourth year of Jishō, the capital was suddenly relocated,[9] confounding everyone. One generally hears it said that this city has been the capital since it was so designated in the time of Emperor Saga,[10] more than four hundred years ago. It should never have been moved arbitrarily on a casual whim like that, and it was only too natural that everyone was so distressed and anxious.

But complaints availed them nothing; everyone, from the emperor to his ministers and nobles, was obliged to move. And how could any among those in attendance at the palace choose to remain back there alone in the old capital? Those hoping to advance their rank and position, those who relied on the emperor's support, strove to make the move as soon as possible, while others, who had missed their moment, had been passed over in life and could hope for no advancement, stayed behind and grieved.

As the days passed, ruin fell upon those fine houses with their jostling throng of roofs. The buildings were dismantled and floated down the Yodo,[11] and before our eyes the land turned to cropping fields. Tastes changed – now everyone prized only the horse and saddle, and the ox and carriage went quite unused.[12] Now property on the south-west seaboard was sought after, while no one cared for estates to the north or east.[13]

At around this time I happened to have reason to visit the new capital, so I went down to Settsu. Looking around, I noted that the area was too cramped to be sectioned off into proper wards. To the north the land rose steeply up to mountains,[14] while to the south it sloped straight down to the nearby sea. There was a constant crash of waves, and a fierce offshore wind blew. The imperial palace stood back in the hills, and was rather reminiscent of how the old Log Palace[15] might have looked, almost charming in its eccentricity.

Where could all those houses be, that had day after day been dismantled and floated downstream in such quantities that they clogged the waterways? Empty plots were everywhere, buildings were few. The old capital was now a ruin, while the new had yet to rise. Every last person felt suspended, unsettled, adrift as floating clouds. The place's former residents lamented the loss of their land. Those who had moved there bewailed the difficulties of building. Along the roads I witnessed men who should by rights travel in a carriage sitting astride a horse, and courtiers who would normally be dressed in court robes wearing instead the new *hitatare*.[16] The old capital's ways had undergone a sudden transformation, and fashions now were indistinguishable from the uncouth country warrior's.

It is said that changes in customs presage times of upheaval, and indeed it was so, for as the days passed all grew increasingly disturbed and restive, until at length the people's grievances bore fruit, and in the winter of that year the capital was returned to its former site. Who knows what happened to all the houses that were dismantled and taken down there, however, for many were never restored.

It is told that in the days of the wise rulers of old the land was governed with compassion – the eaves of the reed-thatched palace roofs were left untrimmed, and if the emperor saw only a thin trail of smoke rising from his people's cooking fires, he excused them payment of even the stipulated taxes. This was because these rulers were given to benevolence and service to their people. We need only compare our present age to theirs to see the difference.

Again, around the Yōwa era[17] I believe it was, although so much time has passed that I no longer quite remember, there was a terrible two-year famine in the world. Drought in spring and summer, typhoons and floods in autumn – disaster followed on disaster, and all the crops failed. In vain did people till the fields in spring[18] and plant in summer; autumn and winter brought no bustling harvest, no storing up of food.

All this drove people throughout the provinces to leave their land and migrate elsewhere, or desert their homes and simply take to the hills. Various prayers to the gods were instigated and fervent Buddhist ceremonies performed at the palace, but to no avail. All the capital's many activities essentially depended on the countryside, and once provisions ceased to arrive, what hope was there of keeping up even a semblance of normalcy? People were driven to offer all their treasured possessions to buyers for a song, but no one would so much as glance at them. And if any exchange did happen to be made, money meant almost nothing, while grain was everything. Beggars crowded the roadsides, and the sound of their wailing filled the ears.

So the first year drew somehow to a close. We hoped for recovery in the new year, but instead a plague was added to our woes, and every semblance of the old life was now gone. All despaired,[19] and we were like fish in a fast-drying pond as calamity tightened its grip on the world from day to day. Finally, those who still looked reasonably presentable took to the streets, clad in hats and leggings, going from door to door, desperately begging. These miserable wretches could be seen staggering along one minute and fallen the next. Countless numbers starved to death by walls and on roadsides. None knew how to dispose of all these corpses; the air was filled with their stench, and one could only avert the eyes from the frequent sight of slowly decomposing bodies. As for the dry river bed,[20] the bodies lay so thick that there was no room for horses and carts to pass.

The poor wood-cutters and other common folk could no longer carry wood from exhaustion, so even fuel became scarce in the city, and those who had nowhere else to turn were reduced to tearing down their own houses and selling the wood in the marketplace. It was said that the price for what a man could carry there would not even keep him alive a day. Strangely, among the wood sold for fuel one saw some with touches of cinnabar or gold leaf – on enquiry, I learned that some as a last resort were going to run-down old temples, stealing the Buddhist images, dismantling the decorative woodwork in the worship hall and breaking these up to sell. Born into these vile latter days,[21] it has been my lot to witness such heartbreaking things.

And I saw other pitiful things besides. Where a man could not bear to part from his wife, or a woman loved her husband dearly, it was always the one whose love was the deeper who died first – in their sympathy for the other they would put themselves second, and give their partner any rare morsel that came their way. So also, if parent and child lived together the parent was always the first to die; a baby would still lie suckling, unaware that its mother was dead.

A monk by the name of Ryūgyō Hōin from Ninnaji,[22] sorrowing to see people dying in such countless numbers, took to inscribing the sacred Sanskrit syllable 'A'[23] on the forehead of any he met with, to lead them to rebirth in paradise. When a count was made of all the dead, the total for the fourth and fifth months came to over 42,300 in the area from Ichijō south and from Kujō north, from East Kyōgoku west and Shujaku east.[24] Of course there were many who died before and after this time, and if all the outlying areas such as the Kamo riverbed, Shirakawa and the Nishi no Kyō[25] were added in, the numbers would be incalculable – and how much more so with the provinces beyond!

Such things also happened, I have heard, in the reign of Emperor Sutoku back in the Chōshō era,[26] but I know nothing of the experience of those times. What I have seen with my own eyes was certainly strange and dreadful.

Also around the same time, as I recall,[27] there was a great earthquake, and a quite exceptional one it was. Mountainsides collapsed, damming the streams, and the sea tilted up and flooded over the land. Water gushed from the rent earth, great rocks split asunder and tumbled into the valleys below. Boats rowing offshore were tossed in the waves, while horses lost their footing on the roads. Not a single temple building or pagoda around the capital remained intact. Some collapsed, others leaned and fell. Like thick plumes of smoke, the dust rose. The roar of shuddering earth and the crash of buildings resounded like thunder.

Anyone indoors was sure to be crushed, but we rushed out only to find the earth split open at our feet. Lacking wings, there could be no escaping to the air. Had we only been dragons, we might have fled to the clouds! Among all the terrors, I realized then, the most terrifying is an earthquake.

The dreadful shaking soon ceased, but the aftershocks continued for some time. Not a day passed without twenty or thirty tremors, of a strength that would normally seem startlingly strong. Finally, ten or twenty days later, the intervals between them lengthened – it would be four or five times a day, then two or three, then every second day, then once in two or three. All told, the aftershocks must have been felt for around three months.

Of the four elements,[28] water, fire and wind commonly inflict harm, while earth causes no great disruptions. Back in the old days, perhaps in the Saikō era,[29] there was a great earthquake that knocked off the head of the buddha of Tōdaiji Temple[30] and caused tremendous damage, but it was not as bad as this.

At the time, all spoke of how futile everything was in the face of life's uncertainties, and their hearts seemed for a while a little less clouded by worldliness, but time passed, and now, years later, no one so much as mentions that time.

Yes, take it for all in all, this world is a hard place to live, and both we and our dwellings are fragile and impermanent, as these events reveal. And besides, there are the countless occasions when situation or circumstance cause us anguish.

Imagine you are someone of no account, who lives next to a powerful man. There may be something that deeply delights you, but you cannot go ahead and express your joy. If something has brought you terrible grief, you cannot raise your voice and weep. You worry over your least action and tremble with every move you make, like a sparrow close to a falcon's nest. Or take a poor man who lives next to a rich one. Ashamed at the sorry sight he makes, he is forever cringing obsequiously before his neighbour as he comes and goes. He must witness his wife and children and his servants filled with envy, and have to hear how the neighbour despises him, and each fresh thought will unsettle him so that he has not a moment's tranquillity.

If you live in a cramped city area, you cannot escape disaster when a fire springs up nearby. If you live in some remote place, commuting to and fro is filled with problems, and you are in constant danger from thieves. A powerful man will be beset by cravings, one without family ties will be scorned. Wealth brings great anxiety, while with poverty come fierce resentments. Dependence on others puts you in their power, while care for others will snare you in the worldly attachments of affection. Follow the social rules, and they hem you in; fail to do so, and you are thought as good as crazy.

Where can one be, what can one do, to find a little safe shelter in this world, and a little peace of mind?

I came into house and property through my paternal grandmother, and lived there for many years. Later, my ties with the place were broken, I came down in the world and, for all my fond memories, I eventually had to leave my home. Past thirty, I chose to build another little house.

It was a mere tenth the size of my former home. I built only a single dwelling for myself; there was no means to add any decent outbuildings.[31] I managed to put a wall around it, but funds did not stretch to a front gate. I used bamboo as the frame for a shed to hold the carriage.[32] Things were always far from safe whenever snow fell or the wind blew. The place was near the river so was in deep danger of flooding, and robbers were a source of constant worry.

All told, I spent some thirty troubled years[33] withstanding the vagaries of this world. At each new setback, I understood afresh how wretched my luck is. And so, in the spring of my fiftieth year, I came to leave my home and take the tonsure, and turned my back on the world.[34] I had never had wife and children, so there were no close ties that were difficult to break. I had no rank and salary to forgo. What was there to hold me to the world? I made my bed among the clouds of Ōhara's mountains,[35] and there I passed five fruitless years.

*

Now at sixty,[36] with the dew of life about to fade, I have fashioned for myself another dwelling to hold me for these final years. I am, if you will, like a traveller who throws up a shelter for the night, or an old silkworm spinning his cocoon. It is not a hundredth the size of the house of my middle years. As I complained my way through life, each passing year has added to my age, and each move reduced my dwelling.

This house looks quite unlike a normal one. It is a mere ten feet square, and less than seven feet high. Since I was not much concerned about where I lived, I did not construct the house to fit the site. I simply set up a foundation, put up a bit of a roof and fastened each joint with a metal catch, so that if I didn't care for one place I could easily move to another. Just how much trouble would it be to rebuild, after all? The house would take a mere two cartloads to shift, and the only expense would be the carrier.

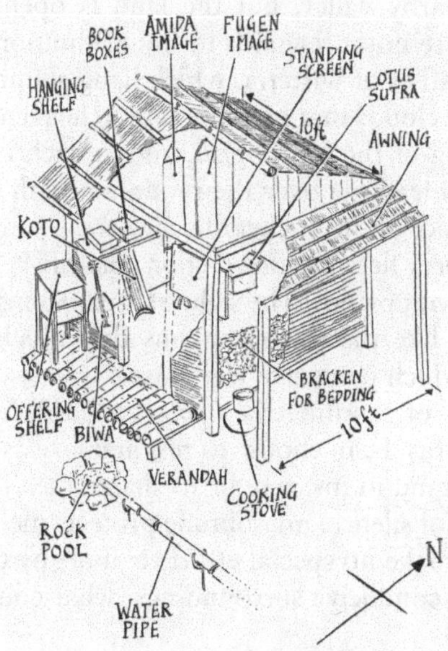

Since retiring here to Mount Hino, I have added a three-foot awning on the east side of my hut, beneath which to store firewood and cook. On the south I put up a veranda of bamboo slats, with an offerings shelf at its western end.[37] Inside there is a standing screen dividing off the north-west section of the room, where I have set up a painted image of Amida with another of the bodhisattva Fugen hung next to it, and a copy of *The Lotus Sutra* placed before them.[38] At the room's eastern edge I have spread a tangle of bracken to serve as bed. A shelf hangs from the ceiling in the south-west corner, holding three black leather boxes that contain extracts from the poetic anthologies, musical treatises, *Essentials of Salvation*[39] and so forth. Beside this stand one *koto* and one *biwa*. The *koto* is the folding kind, the *biwa* has a detachable neck.[40] Such is my temporary abode.

As for its surroundings, to the south is a bamboo water pipe, and I have placed rocks there to make a pool. The forest is close by the house, so I am not short of brushwood to gather. The name of the place is Toyama.[41] Vines cover the paths, trees throng the nearby valley, but the land is open to the west. Indeed there are not a few aids to my meditations. In spring I gaze upon swathes of wisteria, which hang shining in the west like the purple clouds that bear the soul to heaven.[42] In summer I hear the song of the *hototogisu*, and at each call he affirms his promise to lead me over the mountain path of death.[43] In autumn the voice of the cricket fills my ears, a sound that seems to sorrow over a fleeting life so soon cast off.[44] In winter, the snow fills me with pathos. The sight of it piling high only to melt and vanish is like the mounting sins that block our path to redemption, which penitence will erase.

When I tire of chanting the *nenbutsu*[45] and feel disinclined to read the sutras, I can choose to rest and laze as I wish. There is no one to stand in my way or to shame me. Though I have taken no vow of silence, my solitude protects me from the evils of speech.[46] I make no special effort to abide by the precepts,[47] but with such conducive surroundings, what could lead me to break them?

On mornings when my thoughts turn to the 'white retreating waves' of this transient life, I gaze out to the boats that ply the river at Okanoya, and savour as my own the feelings of the old poet Novice Mansei.[48] On evenings when the wind rustles in the leaves of the *katsura* trees, I cast my thoughts back to Xunyang Inlet, and pluck my *biwa* in the way of Tsunenobu.[49] And if the mood is still upon me, often I play to the sough of wind in the pines the piece called 'Autumn Wind Music', or 'Flowing Spring'[50] to the murmur of running water. My skill is poor, but then I do not aim to please the ears of others. I play alone, I sing alone, simply for my own fulfilment.

There is a little brushwood shack at the foot of the mountain, the home of the local warden. He has a little boy who sometimes comes to visit, and in idle hours I go off rambling with him. He is ten, I am sixty – a vast difference in age, yet we find our pleasure in the same things. We pick the seed-heads of grasses, collect rock-pear berries, gather mountain yams or pluck wild parsley. At other times we might go down to the rice fields, to glean the fallen ears of rice and sheave them up. If the day is fine we scramble up to the peak and gaze off to the skies of the capital, my old home, or look out over Mount Kohata, Fushimi Village, Toba and Hatsukashi.[51] No one owns a splendid view, so nothing prevents the heart's delight in it.

If the walk is not too much for me, and I feel inclined to go further afield, I follow the ridgeline over Mount Sumi and Kasadori to pay my respects at Iwama or Ishiyama Temples.[52] At other times, I might go on over the plain of Awazu to call on Semimaru's old site, or cross Tanakami River to visit the grave of Sarumaro.[53] On my way back, depending on the season, I may linger over the cherry blossoms, search out the autumn leaves, pluck young fern shoots or gather nuts as I go, as offerings for the altar or as gifts to take home.

On quiet nights, the moon at my window recalls to me past friends, and tears wet my sleeve at the cries of the monkeys.[54] The fireflies in the nearby grass blend their little lights with the fishermen's fires of distant Makinoshima; the sound of dawn rain comes to me like a storm wind in the treetops.[55] When I hear the soft cry of the pheasant, it seems to me my own father or mother;[56] the mountain deer that have learned to come so close reveal to me how distant from the world I have become.

There are times when I stir the embers of my fire to keep me company in the wakefulness of old age. There is nothing to fear from this mountain – the owl's cry is poignant to my ears, and through the seasons I never tire of the mountain's moving beauties. And for one who thought and understood more deeply still than I, this place would surely hold yet greater joys.

When I first came to live here, I thought my time would be brief, but already five years have passed. This passing shelter of mine has slowly become a home; the eaves are deep in rotting leaves, moss covers the foundations.

When news of the capital happens to come my way, I learn of many people in high places who have met their end since I retired to this mountain, and other lesser folk besides, too many to be told. And how many houses, too, have been lost in all those fires? In all this, my mere passing shelter has remained tranquil and safe from fears.

Small it may be, but there is a bed to sleep on at night, and a place to sit in the daytime. As a simple place to house myself, it lacks nothing. The hermit crab prefers a little shell for his home. He knows what the world holds. The osprey chooses the wild shoreline, and this is because he fears mankind. And I too am the same. Knowing what the world holds and its ways, I desire nothing from it, nor chase after its prizes. My one craving is to be at peace, my one pleasure to live free of troubles.

People do not always build a house with the important things in mind. Some will build for wife and children or for the wider household, others for their intimates and friends. Some may build for their master or their teacher, or even for their possessions or their oxen and horses. But I have built this house for my own self and for no one else. And this is because, the world being what it is, and the way I am now, I have no one who shares my life, nor any servants to work for me. Who would I put in a larger house if I built one, after all?

People who cultivate friendships prize men with wealth, and prefer those who are eager to please. They do not always cherish friends who are loving, or pure of heart. Best by far is the company of flute and strings, and of the flowers and moon. Servants and retainers crave endless rewards, and love a master who showers them with favours. They have no interest in affectionate concern or a calm and peaceful life. Better far to be your own servant. How? If something needs doing, use yourself to do it. It may be tiring, but it is easier than employing another and troubling yourself over him. If you need to go somewhere, walk yourself. You may grow weary, but better far than worrying over horse and saddle, oxen and cart.

These days, I divide myself into two uses – these hands are my servants, these feet my transport. They serve me just as I wish. Mind knows when things feel hard for the body; at such times it will grant the body rest, and work it when it is willing. Yet, work the body though it does, the mind will never push too far, and if the body is reluctant, this will not perturb the mind. Indeed the habit of walking and working is good for the health. Why sit idly about, after all? It is a sin to bring trouble to others. Why should I borrow another's strength?

So too with food and clothing. Be it robe of vine fibre[57] or hempen quilt, I cover myself in whatever comes to hand, and keep myself alive with wild asters[58] from the fields and nuts from the mountains. Since I do not mix with others, shame causes me no regrets. Plain fare tastes all the better when food is scarce.

I do not make claims for these pleasures to disparage the rich. I am simply comparing my past life with my present one. The Triple World is solely Mind.[59] Without a peaceful mind, elephants, horses and the seven treasures are worthless things, palaces and fine towers mean nothing.

I love my tiny hut, my lonely dwelling. When I chance to go down into the capital, I am ashamed of my lowly beggar status, but once back here again I pity those who chase after the sordid rewards of the world. If any doubt my words, let them look to the fish and the birds. Fish never tire of water, a state incomprehensible to any but the fish. The bird's desire for the forest makes sense to none but birds. And so it is with the pleasure of seclusion. Who but one who lives it can understand its joys?

Like the moon that hangs above the mountain rim, my life now tilts towards its close. Soon I will enter the darkness of the Three Paths.[60] What point is there in mulling over past actions?

The Buddha's essential teaching is to relinquish all attachment. This fondness for my hut I now see must be error, and my attachment to a life of seclusion and peace is an impediment to rebirth. How could I waste my days like this, describing useless pleasures?

In the quiet dawn I ponder this, and question my own heart: you fled the world to live among forest and mountain in order to discipline the mind and practise the Buddhist Way. But though you have all the trappings of a holy man, your heart is corrupt. Your dwelling may aspire to be the hut of the holy Vimilakīrti himself, but the practice you maintain in it cannot match even that of the fool Śuddhipanthaka.[61] Have you after all let the poverty ordained by past sins distract you? Or have your delusions tipped you over into madness?

When I confront my heart thus, it cannot reply. At most, this mortal tongue can only end in three faltering invocations of the holy, unapproachable name of Amida.[62]

Written in his hut on Toyama at the close of the third month in the second year of Kenryaku, by the monk Ren'in.[63]

ESSAYS IN IDLENESS

Preface

What strange folly, to beguile the tedious hours like this all day before my ink stone, jotting down at random the idle thoughts that cross my mind . . .

I

To be born into this world of ours, it seems, brings with it so much to long for.

The rank of emperor is, of course, unspeakably exalted; even his remotest descendants fill one with awe, having sprung from no mere human seed.[1]

Needless to say, the great ruler,[2] and even the lesser nobles who are granted attendant guards to serve them,[3] are also thoroughly magnificent. Their children and grandchildren too are still impressive, even if they have come down in the world. As for those of lesser degree, although they may make good according to their rank, and put on airs and consider themselves special, they are really quite pathetic.

No one could be less enviable than a monk. Sei Shōnagon[4] wrote that people treat them like unfeeling lumps of wood, and this is perfectly true. And there is nothing impressive about the way those with power will throw their weight around. As the holy man Sōga,[5] I think, remarked, fame and fortune are an affliction for a monk, and violate the Buddha's teachings.

There is much to admire, though, in a dedicated recluse.

It is most important to present well, in both appearance and bearing. One never tires of spending time with someone whose speech is attractive and pleasing to the ear, and who does not talk overmuch. There is nothing worse than when someone you thought impressive reveals himself as lacking in sensibility. Status and personal appearance are things one is born with, after all, but surely the inner man can always be improved with effort. It is a great shame to see a fine upstanding fellow fall in with low and ugly types who easily run rings round him, and all for want of cultivation and learning.

A man should learn the orthodox literature,[6] write poetry in Chinese as well as Japanese, and study music, and should ideally also be a model to others in his familiarity with ceremonial court customs and precedents. He should write a smooth, fair hand, carry the rhythm well when songs are sung at banquets,[7] and when offered sake, make a show of declining it but nevertheless be able to drink.

2

A ruler who forgets the ways of the great emperors of old,[8] who cares nothing for the woes of the people or the decay of the state but instead takes pride in luxurious indulgence and generally throws his weight around in high-handed fashion, is actually making a great fool of himself.

As the Kujō Minister of the Right wrote in his *Precepts*,[9] 'In all things, from court costume to horses and carriages, use what is to hand. Never strive for beauty.' Retired Emperor Juntoku also wrote concerning court procedures, 'The emperor should clothe himself simply.'[10]

3

No matter how splendid in every way, there is something dreadfully lacking in a man who does not pursue the art of love. He is, to coin the old phrase, like a beautiful wine cup that lacks a base.[11]

The elegant thing is for a lover to wander aimlessly hither and yon, drenched with the frosts or dews of night, tormented by fears of his parents' reproaches and the censure of the world, the heart beset with uncertainties, yet for all that sleeping often alone, though always fitfully.

On the other hand, he shouldn't lose himself to love too thoroughly, or gain the reputation of being putty in women's hands.

4

It is an admirable thing in a man to keep his mind on the world to come, and remain heedful of the Buddhist path.

5

A man who meets with misfortune and sorrow should not shave his head and become a monk on impulse; he does better to quietly shut his gate and seclude himself unobtrusively, expecting nothing of each passing day.

Counsellor Akimoto[12] is reputed to have wished to 'gaze upon the moon in blameless exile'. Precisely so.

6

It is better for even the high-born, not to mention those of lowly station, to have no children.

Prince Kaneakira, the Kujō Chief Minister and the Hanazono Minister of the Left[13] all wished to see their line die out. The Somedono Minister also remarked in *The Tale of Yotsugi*,[14] 'It is best to have no descendants – it is most unfortunate when they prove inferior to their forebears.' Prince Shōtoku[15] too, when having his own tomb prepared, is reputed to have ordered that it be 'trimmed here and cut back there, for I aim to leave no descendants'.

7

If our life did not fade and vanish like the dews of Adashino's graves or the drifting smoke from Toribe's burning grounds,[16] but lingered on for ever, how little the world would move us. It is the ephemeral nature of things that makes them wonderful.

Among all living creatures, it is man that lives longest. The brief dayfly dies before evening; summer's cicada knows neither spring nor autumn. What a glorious luxury it is to taste life to the full for even a single year. If you constantly regret life's passing, even a thousand long years will seem but the dream of a night.

Why cling to a life which cannot last for ever, only to arrive at ugly old age? The longer you live, the greater your share of shame. It is most seemly to die before forty at the latest.[17] Once past this age, people develop an urge to mix with others without the least shame at their own unsightliness; they spend their dwindling years fussing adoringly over their children and grandchildren, hoping to live long enough to see them make good in the world. Their greed for the things of this world grows ever deeper, till they lose all ability to be moved by life's pathos, and become really quite disgraceful.

8

Nothing so distracts the human heart as sexual desire. How foolish men's hearts are!

Aroma, for instance, is a mere transient thing, yet a whiff of delightful incense from a woman's robes will always excite a man, though he knows perfectly well that it is just a passing effect of robe-smoking.[18]

The wizard priest of Kume[19] is said to have lost his supernatural powers when he spied the white legs of a woman as she squatted washing clothes. I can quite believe it – after all, the beautiful, plump, glowing flesh of a woman's arm or leg is quite a different matter from some artificial allurement.

9

Beautiful hair on a woman will draw a man's gaze – but we can judge what manner of person she is and the nature of her sensibility even by simply hearing her speak from behind a screen.

A mere unintended glimpse of a woman can distract a man's heart; and if a woman sleeps fitfully, and is prepared to endure impossible difficulties heedless of her own well-being, it is all because her mind is on love.

Yes indeed, the ways of love lie deep in us. Many are the allurements of our senses, yet we can distance ourselves from them all. But among them this one alone seems without exception to plague us all, young and old, wise and foolish.

So it is that we have those tales of how a woman's hair can snare and hold even an elephant, or how the rutting stag of autumn will always be drawn by the sound of a flute made from the wood of a woman's shoe.[20]

We must discipline ourselves to be constantly prudent and vigilant lest we fall into this trap.

10

Though a home is of course merely a transient habitation,[21] a place that is set up in beautiful taste to suit its owner is a delightful thing.

Even the moonlight is so much the more moving when it shines into a house where a refined person dwells in tranquil elegance. There is nothing fashionable or showy about the place, it is true, yet the grove of trees is redolent of age, the plants in the carefully untended garden carry a hint of delicate feelings, while the veranda and open-weave fence are tastefully done, and inside the house the casually disposed things have a tranquil, old-fashioned air. It is all most refined.

How ugly and depressing to see a house that has employed a bevy of craftsmen to work everything up to a fine finish, where all the household items set out for proud display are rare and precious foreign or Japanese objects, and where even the plants in the garden are clipped and contorted rather than left to grow as they will. How could anyone live for long in such a place? The merest glimpse will provoke the thought that all this could go up in smoke in an instant.

Yes, on the whole you can tell a great deal about the owner from his home.

The Later Tokudaiji Minister[22] once had rope strung over the roof of the main house to stop the kites from roosting on it. 'What could be wrong with having kites on your roof? This shows what manner of man he is!' exclaimed the poet-monk Saigyō,[23] and it is said he never called there again. I was reminded of this story when I noticed once that Prince Ayanokōji[24] had laid rope over his Kosaka residence. Someone told me, however, that it was because he pitied the frogs in his pond when he observed how crows gathered on the roof to catch them. I was most impressed. Perhaps the Tokudaiji Minister too might have had some such reason for acting as he did?

11

One day in the tenth month, I went to call on someone in a remote mountain village beyond Kurusuno.[25]

Making my way along the mossy path, I came at length to the lonely hut where he lived. There was not a sound except for the soft drip of water from a bamboo pipe buried deep in fallen leaves. The vase on the altar shelf with its haphazard assortment of chrysanthemums and sprigs of autumn leaves bespoke someone's presence.

Moved, I said to myself, 'One could live like this' – but my mood was then somewhat spoiled by noticing at the far end of the garden a large mandarin tree, branches bowed with fruit, that was firmly protected by a stout fence. If only that tree weren't there! I thought.

12

What happiness to sit in intimate conversation with someone of like mind, warmed by candid discussion of the amusing and fleeting ways of this world . . . but such a friend is hard to find, and instead you sit there doing your best to fit in with whatever the other is saying, feeling deeply alone.

There is some pleasure to be had from agreeing with the other in general talk that interests you both, but it's better if he takes a slightly different position from yours. 'No, I can't agree with that,' you'll say to each other combatively, and you'll fall into arguing the matter out. This sort of lively discussion is a pleasant way to pass the idle hours, but in fact most people tend to grumble about things different from oneself, and though you can put up with the usual boring platitudes, such men are far indeed from the true friend after your own heart, and leave you feeling quite forlorn.[26]

13

It is a most wonderful comfort to sit alone beneath a lamp, book spread before you,[27] and commune with someone from the past whom you have never met.

As to books – those moving volumes of *Wenxuan*, the *Wenji* of Bai Juyi, the words of Laozi and *Zhuangzi*.[28] There are many moving works from our own land, too, by scholars of former times.

14

Japanese poetry[29] is a most delightful thing. The doings of lowly folk, mountain woodsmen and so forth are beguiling when expressed in poetry, and even the terrifying wild boar becomes quite tamed and elegant by the phrase 'where the wild boar lays his head'.[30]

Some of today's poems could be said to achieve a nice turn of phrase here and there, but somehow they just do not have the old poetry's subtle flavour of feeling that resonates beyond the words.

Ki no Tsurayuki's 'No twining thread my heart' in the *Kokinshū*[31] is said to be mere dross, but I do not think any poet today could match it. So many poems of that time have a similar sort of cast and language to this. It is hard to see why people should single out Tsurayuki's poem for criticism. In *The Tale of Genji*[32] the second line is given slightly differently.

The same is said of the *Shinkokinshū* poem 'Even the sole

pine is lonely on its peak',[33] and it's true, one could find the cast of it a little awkward. Yet Ienaga[34] records in his diary that the poem was judged to be good in a poetry competition, and His Majesty[35] spoke of it later as particularly impressive.

It is sometimes said that the Way of Japanese poetry alone has remained unchanged since the old days – but I wonder. The old poetic words and epithets that people today still use in poetry have a different ring from those same words in the poems of earlier poets. The old poems were simple and unaffected, and had a purity and beauty of cast and great depth of feeling.

There is also much moving language in the songs of the *Ryōjin hishō*.[36]

Somehow, even the most casual words of those from earlier times have an impressive ring to them.

15

Going on a journey, whatever the destination, makes you feel suddenly awake and alive to everything.

There are so many new things to see in rustic places and country villages as you wander about looking. It is also delightful to send word to those back home in the capital asking for news, and adding reminders to be sure and see to this or that matter.

In such places, you are particularly inclined to be attentive to all you see. You even notice the fine quality of things you've brought with you, and someone's artistic talents or beauty will delight you more than they usually would.

Withdrawing quietly to a retreat at a temple or shrine is also delightful.

16

Kagura[37] is wonderfully refined and elegant.

As to musical instruments in general, the flute and the little *hichiriki* have the best tone. And one is always happy to hear the *biwa* and the six-stringed *koto*.[38]

17

When you are on a retreat at a mountain temple, concentrating on your devotions, the hours are never tedious, and the heart feels cleansed and purified.

18

It is an excellent thing to live modestly, shun luxury and wealth and not lust after fame and fortune. Rare has been the wise man who was rich.

In China once there was a man by the name of Xu You,[39] who owned nothing and even drank directly from his cupped hands. Seeing this, someone gave him a 'singing gourd'[40] to use as a cup; he hung it in a tree, but when he heard it singing in the wind one day he threw it away, annoyed by the noise it made, and went back to drinking his water from his hands. What a free, pure spirit!

Sun Chen had no bedclothes to sleep under in the winter months, only a bundle of straw which he slept in at night and put away again each morning.

The Chinese wrote these stories to hand down to later times because they found them so impressive. No one bothers to tell such tales in our country.

19

The changing seasons are moving in every way.

Everyone seems to feel that 'it is above all autumn that moves the heart to tears',[41] and there is some truth in this, yet surely it is spring that stirs the heart more profoundly. Then, birdsong is full of the feel of spring, the plants beneath the hedges bud into leaf in the warm sunlight, the slowly deepening season brings soft mists, while the blossoms at last begin to open, only to meet with ceaseless winds and rain that send them flurrying restlessly to earth. Until the leaves appear on the boughs, the heart is endlessly perturbed.

The scented flowering orange is famously evocative, but it is above all plum blossom that has the power to carry you back to moments of cherished memory.[42] The exquisite kerria, the hazy clusters of wisteria blossom – all these things linger in the heart.

Someone has said that at the time of the Buddha's birthday and the Kamo festival[43] in the fourth month, when the trees are cool with luxuriant new leaf, one is particularly moved by the pathos of things and by a longing for others, and indeed it is true. And who could not be touched to melancholy in the fifth month, when the sweet flag iris leaves are laid on roofs,[44] and the rice seedlings are planted out, and the water rail's knocking call is heard? The sixth month is also moving, with white evening-glory blooming over the walls of poor dwellings, and the smoke from smouldering smudge fires. The purifications of the sixth month[45] are also delightful.

The festival of Tanabata[46] is wonderfully elegant. Indeed so many things happen together in autumn – the nights grow slowly more chill, wild geese come crying over, and when the bush clover begins to yellow the early rice is harvested and hung to dry. The morning after a typhoon has blown through is also delightful.

Writing this, I realize that all this has already been spoken of long ago in *The Tale of Genji* and *The Pillow Book* – but that is no reason not to say it again. After all, things thought but left unsaid only fester inside you. So I let my brush run on like this for my own foolish solace; these pages deserve to be torn up and discarded, after all, and are not something others will ever see.

To continue – the sight of a bare wintry landscape is almost as lovely as autumn. It is delightful to see fallen autumn leaves scattered among the plants by the water's edge, or vapour rising from the garden stream[47] on a morning white with frost. It is also especially moving to observe everyone bustling about at year's end, preparing for the new year. And then there is the forlornly touching sight of the waning moon around the twentieth day, hung in a clear, cold sky, although people consider it too dreary to look at.[48] The Litany of Buddha Names and the Presentation of Tributes[49] are thoroughly moving and magnificent, and in fact all the numerous court ceremonies and events at around this time, taking place as they do amidst the general end-of-year bustle, present an impressive sight. The way the Worship of the Four Directions follows so quickly upon the Great Demon Expulsion[50] is wonderful too.

In the thick darkness of New Year's Eve,[51] people light pine torches and rush about, so fast that their feet virtually skim the ground, making an extraordinary racket for some reason, and knocking on everyone's doors until late at night – but then at last around dawn all grows quiet, and you savour the touching moment of saying farewell to the old year. I was moved to find that in the East they still perform the ritual for dead souls[52] on the night when the dead are said to return, although these days this has ceased to be done in the capital.

And so, watching the new year dawn in the sky, you are stirred by a sense of utter newness, although the sky looks no different from yesterday's. It is also touching to see the happy sight of new year pines[53] gaily decorating the houses all along the main streets.

20

A certain recluse monk once remarked, 'I have relinquished all that ties me to the world, but the one thing that still haunts me is the beauty of the sky.' I can quite see why he would feel this.

21

You can find solace for all things by looking at the moon. Someone once declared that there is nothing more delightful than the moon, while another disagreed, claiming that dew is the most moving – a charming debate. Surely there is nothing that isn't moving, in fact, depending on circumstance.

Not only the moon and blossoms, but the wind in particular can stir people's hearts.

The sight of a clear stream breaking against rocks is always delightful, whatever the season.

I was truly moved when I read the words of the Chinese poem that run, 'Day and night, the Yuan and Xiang go flowing ever east, / never pausing for a grieving man.'[54] Then there is Xi Kang, who wrote how, roving among mountain and stream, his heart delighted to see the fish and birds.[55] Nothing provides such balm for the heart as wandering somewhere far from the world of men, in a place of pure water and fresh leaf.

22

One yearns for the old world in every way. Modern fashions just seem to grow more and more vulgar.

The most beautiful finely crafted wooden utensils are those from the old days. As for letters, those old ones on reused scraps are written in wonderful language. Everyday speech is also going from bad to worse. Someone who remembers the old days once remarked, 'Back then, people used to say "lift the carriage" or "raise the flame", but now it is always "lift up the carriage" and "raise up the flame".[56] It is also a great shame the way that instead of the old "groundsmen to the standing lights" people now say "light up the lamps", and they will insist on shortening the Imperial Audience Chamber for the Sutra Lectures to simply "The Imperial Lecture Room".'[57]

23

For all the falling off of these latter days, the sublime Ninefold Palace[58] still remains marvellously unsullied by the world.

Places such as the Dew Platform and the Imperial Breakfast Room, or Such-and-such Hall or Gate, have a splendid ring to them, while even names such as *kojitomi, koitajiki* or *takayarido*,[59] which can refer to things found in the houses of commoners as well, sound wonderful.

'All in place for the night watch in the Gallery!' is a marvellous phrase. The call 'Haste to the lamps!' when the lights are to be lit in the Imperial Bedchamber is also wonderful. The spectacle of the leader directing the assembled nobles in palace ceremonies, and the smug faces of the lesser officials who are so used to taking part in these things, are also enjoyable. It is also amusing to witness them dozing off in corners during ceremonies on those long, cold nights.

The Tokudaiji Minister[60] once remarked that the bell rung in the Sacred Mirror Room[61] has a most marvellous and elegant sound.

24

The seclusion of the high priestess at Nonomiya was a most refined and delightful thing.[62] It is also interesting that she must avoid Buddhist words such as 'sutra' or 'the Buddha', replacing them with 'child within' and 'dyed paper'.[63]

All shrines to the gods have a compelling air of refinement. There is something quite special about the sight of the venerable old shrine groves, and the sacred fences surrounding the shrines themselves, and the way sacred paper streamers are tied to the boughs of the *sakaki* tree,[64] are quite splendid.

The most delightful shrines are: Ise, Kamo, Kasuga, Hirano, Sumiyoshi, Miwa, Kibune, Yoshida, Ōharano, Matsuo and Umenomiya.[65]

25

This world is changeable as the deeps and shallows of Asuka River[66] – time passes, what was here is gone, joy and grief visit by turns, once splendid places change to abandoned wastelands, and even the same house as of old is now home to different people. The peach and the plum tree utter nothing – with whom can we speak of past things?[67] Still more moving in its transience is the ruin of some fine residence of former times, whose glory we never saw.

It is deeply poignant to see the Kyōgoku-dono and Hōjōji Temple,[68] and witness there the hopes of the man who built them, now so transfigured. The Midōdono[69] created these magnificent buildings and donated many of his estates to the temple, full of plans that his family would continue to act as regents for future emperors and retain its worldly power – could he have dreamed then that an age would come when all that he had set up would lie in such ruin? The temple gates and the Kondō were still standing until recently, but the south gate burned in the Shōwa era.[70] The Kondō later collapsed, and no attempt has been made to rebuild it. Only the Muryōju Hall[71] still stands in its former state, with inside it an awe-inspiring row of nine fifteen-foot-tall images of the Buddha. It is moving, too, to see the calligraphy by Grand Counsellor Kōzei and the doors with Kaneyuki's writing,[72] still clearly visible. The Hokke-dō[73] is apparently still standing as well. For how much longer, I wonder?

In places where such remnants no longer exist, one can sometimes still see foundation stones in the ground, but none now know what buildings these once were.

And so we see how fickle is the world in all things, for those who would plan for a time they will not live to see.

26

How mutable the flower of the human heart, a fluttering blossom gone before the breeze's touch – so we recall the bygone years when the heart of another was our close companion, each dear word that stirred us then still unforgotten; and yet, it is the way of things that the beloved should move into worlds beyond our own, a parting far sadder than from the dead. Thus did Mozi grieve over a white thread that the dye would alter for ever, and at the crossroads Yang Zhu lamented the path's parting ways.[74]

In Retired Emperor Horikawa's collection of one hundred poems,[75] we read:

Where once I called on her	*mukashi mishi*
the garden fence is now in ruins –	*imo ga kakine wa*
flowering there I find	*arenikeri*
only wild violets, woven through	*tsubana majiri no*
with rank spring grasses.	*sumire nomi shite*

Such is the desolate scene that once must have met the poet's eye.

27

There is nothing more forlorn than that moment in the emperor's abdication ceremony[76] when the sacred sword, the seal of state and the sacred mirror are passed across.

In the spring after his abdication, the newly retired emperor composed the following.

The palace groundsmen	*tonomori no*
have turned away from me	*tomo no miyakko*
leaving these grounds unswept	*yoso ni shite*
where now the falling blossoms	*harawanu niwa ni*
carpet the earth.[77]	*hana zo chirishiku*

How wretched he must have felt, when all their busy duties for the new emperor distracted them from coming. Such moments reveal our hearts.

28

Nothing is more affecting than the emperor's year of mourning for a parent.[78]

It is all so dismal – the mourning hut, with its lowered floor, coarse cloth replacing the usual brocade along the top of crude reed blinds, rough furnishings, and everyone in attendance wearing clothes that are much more austere than usual, even down to the different scabbard and its ornamental cord.

29

At times of quiet contemplation, my one irresistible emotion is an aching nostalgia for all things past.

Everyone is hushed and sleeping, and you are beguiling yourself through the long night hours by tidying away this and that, discarding bits of used writing paper you don't want to keep, when you come upon a page that someone long since dead has used for writing practice or to sketch something, and you suddenly feel yourself back inside that moment. Even if it is a long-ago letter from someone still alive, it is moving to ponder when and in what year you received it.

How melancholy to think that your own familiar things, too, will remain in existence down the years to come, indifferent and unchanged.

30

Nothing is sadder than the aftermath of a death.

How trying it is to be jammed in together in some cramped and inconvenient mountain establishment for the forty-nine-day mourning period, performing the services for the dead.[79] Never have the days passed faster. On the final day everyone is gruff and uncommunicative; each becomes engrossed in the importance of his own tidying and packing, then all go their separate ways. Once home again, the family will face all manner of fresh sorrows.

People go about warning each other of the various things that should be ritually avoided for the sake of the family.[80] What a way to talk, at such a time! Really, what a wretched thing the human heart is!

Even with the passage of time the deceased is in no way forgotten, of course, but 'the dead grow more distant with each day',[81] as the saying goes. And so, for all the memories, it seems our sorrow is no longer as acute as at death, for we begin to chatter idly and laugh again.

The corpse is buried on some deserted mountainside, we visit it only at the prescribed times, and soon moss has covered the grave marker, the grave is buried under fallen leaves, and only the howling evening winds and the moon at night come calling there.

It is all very well while there are those who remember and mourn the dead, but soon they too pass away; the descendants only know of him by hearsay, so they are hardly likely to grieve over his death. Finally, all ceremonies for him cease, no one any longer knows who he was or even his name, and only the grasses of each passing spring grow there to move the sensitive to pity; at length even the graveyard pine that sobbed in stormy winds is cut for firewood before its thousand years are up, the ancient mound is levelled by the plough, and the place becomes a field. The last trace of the grave itself has finally disappeared. It is sad to think of.

31

One morning after a beautiful fall of snow, I had reason to write a letter to an acquaintance, but I omitted to make any mention of the snow. I was delighted when she responded, 'Do you expect me to pay any attention to the words of someone so perverse that he fails to enquire how I find this snowy landscape? What deplorable insensitivity!'

The lady is no longer alive, so I treasure even this trifling memory.

32

Around the twentieth day of the ninth month, someone invited me along to view the moon with him. We wandered and gazed until first light. Along the way, my companion came upon a house he remembered. He had his name announced, and in he went. In the unkempt and dew-drenched garden, a hint of casual incense lingered in the air. It was all movingly redolent of a secluded life.

In due course my companion emerged, but the elegance of the scene led me to stay a little longer and watch from the shadows. Soon the double doors opened a fraction wider; it seemed the lady was gazing at the moon. It would have been very disappointing had she immediately bolted the doors as soon as the visit was over. She could not know that someone would still be watching. Such sensibility could only be the fruit of a habitual attitude of mind.

I heard that this lady died not long after.

33

When the present palace was constructed,[82] it was shown to those who were thoroughly conversant with palace precedent, and pronounced without fault. The day of the imperial move to the new residence was drawing near when the emperor's mother,

Genkimon-in,[83] was shown it, and impressed everyone by pointing out that, in the old palace, the semi-circular 'comb' window in the Kan'in-dono[84] had been rounder and without a frame. The new windows had been given a pointed top, like a leaf-tip, and a wooden frame, so the error was corrected.

34

What we call a *kaikō*[85] is the plug of a shell that is shaped like a conch but smaller, and elongated at the mouth. I saw some once in the bay of Kanesawa in Musashino.[86] The people in those parts call it *henadari*.

35

People with poor handwriting should not hesitate to go ahead and write their own letters. It is tasteless to get someone else to do it for you on the grounds that your writing is terrible.

36

Someone told me the following incident.

'It had been quite some time since I'd called on a certain lady. Aware of my negligence, I was imagining how resentful she would be feeling, and wondering what I could possibly say, when a message came from her asking if I had a servant to spare, and if so might she borrow him. This was quite unexpected and delightful. Such tact and sensibility is a fine thing.' I could quite see why he said so.

37

If someone with whom one constantly shares one's intimate everyday life suddenly becomes reserved and polite in a certain situation, some will no doubt react by saying, 'Why so formal all of a sudden?' It strikes me, however, as a sign of true integrity and excellence of character.

On the other hand, if someone you don't know well opened

up and started talking candidly to you, you would also be favourably impressed.

38

It is foolish to be in thrall to fame and fortune, engaged in painful striving all your life with never a moment of peace and tranquillity.

Great wealth will drive you to neglect your own well-being in pursuit of it. It is asking for harm and tempting trouble. Though you leave behind at your death a mountain of gold high enough to prop up the North Star itself, it will only cause problems for those who come after you. Nor is there any point in all those pleasures that delight the eyes of fools. Big carriages, fat horses, glittering gold and jewels – any man of sensibility would view such things as gross stupidity. Toss your gold away in the mountains; hurl your jewels into the deep. Only a complete fool is led astray by avarice.

Everyone would like to leave their name unburied for posterity – but the high-born and exalted are not necessarily fine people, surely. A dull, stupid person can be born into a good house, attain high status thanks to opportunity and live in the height of luxury, while many wonderfully wise and saintly men choose to remain in lowly positions, and end their days without ever having met with good fortune. A fierce craving for high status and position is next in folly to the lust for fortune.

We long to leave a name for our exceptional wisdom and sensibility – but when you really think about it, desire for a good reputation is merely revelling in the praise of others. Neither those who praise us nor those who denigrate will remain in the world for long, and others who hear their opinions will be gone in short order as well. Just who should we feel ashamed before, then? Whose is the recognition we should crave? Fame in fact attracts abuse and slander. No, there is nothing to be gained from leaving a lasting name. The lust for fame is the third folly.

Let me now say a few words, however, to those who dedicate themselves to the search for knowledge and the desire for understanding. Knowledge leads to deception; talent and ability only serve to increase earthly desires. Knowledge acquired by listening to others or through study is not true knowledge. So what then should we call knowledge? Right and wrong are simply part of a single continuum. What should we call good? One who is truly wise has no knowledge or virtue, nor honour nor fame. Who then will know of him, and speak of him to others? This is not because he hides his virtue and pretends foolishness – he is beyond all distinctions such as wise and foolish, gain and loss.

I have been speaking of what it is to cling to one's delusions and seek after fame and fortune. All things of this phenomenal world are mere illusion. They are worth neither discussing nor desiring.

39

Someone asked the holy priest Hōnen[87] how to prevent himself from being negligent in his practice by inadvertently nodding off when chanting the *nenbutsu*. 'Chant for as long as you are awake,' answered Hōnen. Venerably spoken.

Likewise, Hōnen once said, 'If you are certain of entering paradise at death, your rebirth there is certain. If you are in doubt, your rebirth will be likewise.' This also was venerably said.

He also said, 'Even if you doubt, recite the *nenbutsu* and you will attain rebirth in paradise.' This too was wonderfully spoken.

40

A certain novice monk in Inaba[88] was rumoured to have a beautiful daughter, and many men came asking for her hand. But the girl ate nothing but chestnuts and never touched grains, so her father declared that she was too eccentric to be marriageable, and rejected them all.

41

When I went to see the horse racing at the Kamo Shrine[89] on the fifth day of the fifth month, the view from our carriage was blocked by a throng of common folk. We all got down and moved towards the fence for a better view, but that area was particularly crowded and we couldn't make our way through.

We then noticed a priest who had climbed a chinaberry tree across the way to sit in its fork and watch from there. He was so sleepy as he clung there that he kept nodding off, and only just managed to start awake in time to save himself from falling each time. Those who saw him couldn't believe their eyes. 'What an extraordinary fool!' they all sneered. 'How can a man who's perched up there so precariously among the branches relax so much that he falls asleep?'

A thought suddenly occurred to me. 'Any of us may die from one instant to the next,' I said, 'and in fact we are far more foolish than this priest – here we are, contentedly watching the world go by, oblivious to death.'

'That's so true,' said those in front of me. 'It's really very stupid, isn't it,' and they turned around and invited me in and made room for me.

Anyone can have this sort of insight, but at that particular moment it came as a shock, which is no doubt why people were so struck by it. Humans are not mere insensate beings like trees or rocks, after all, and on occasion things can really strike home.

42

The son of the Karahashi Captain[90] was a priest of considerable rank by the name of Gyōga, who taught doctrinal scholarship. He suffered from dizziness, and as he aged his nose became blocked and he found it increasingly hard to breathe. He tried all manner of cures but it only grew worse – his eyes, brows and forehead swelled hugely and protruded until he could no longer see. He looked like one of those grotesque masks they wear in the Ni no Mai dance,[91] and at length his face grew quite demonic, with eyes near the top of his head and his nose up around his forehead. Once it got to this stage, he hid himself even from the other monks and lived alone, and after many years his condition grew so bad that he died.

Such extraordinary illnesses do exist.

43

One day at the close of spring, when the air is soft and exquisite, you happen upon the house of someone who is evidently of some distinction. The place is large, with an ancient grove of trees, and cherry blossoms drift down in the garden. Unable simply to pass by, you slip into the grounds. The lattice shutters along the southern wall are all lowered, lending it a forlorn air, but you peep in through a torn blind at a half-open door in the eastern wall, and see a handsome youth of around twenty sitting there, relaxed but casually elegant, intent on a book that lies spread on the desk before him.

You long to ask someone who he might have been.

44

From a rough-woven bamboo door a very young man sets forth, tellingly clothed in glowing courtly hunting costume of a colour made indeterminate by moonlight, and deep violet gathered trousers.[92] Accompanied by a little child attendant, he makes his way along a narrow path that winds on through the fields, drenched in dew from the brushing rice plants, and as he goes he plays quite marvellously upon a flute. No one in these parts could appreciate such playing, you think, and intrigued by the scene you follow him, wondering where he might be going. The playing ceases, and he enters the gateway of a noble house at the foot of a hill. Ox carriages stand about, propped on their empty shafts,[93] an arresting sight in this country setting, and you ask one of the servants what is happening. 'Prince Such-and-such is in residence at the moment,' he replies, 'and I believe he is holding a Buddhist service.'

Monks are making their way towards the worship hall. A penetrating scent of incense comes wafting on the chill night breeze. Gentlewomen come and go along the roofed gallery between the main house and the worship hall, the fragrance of their scented robes drifting in their wake – such careful elegance, deep in the country where no eyes could see them.

From the wild and untrimmed 'rough autumn fields'[94] of the garden, heavy with dripping dew and shrill with the plaint of insects, comes the murmur of a garden stream, while the clouds seem to scud more rapidly across the sky than in the city, the moon slipping in and out unpredictably among them.

45

Kinyo no Nii had an elder brother called Abbot Ryōgaku,[95] who was very hot-tempered.

A large hackberry tree grew alongside his hut, so people called him 'the Hackberry Priest'. Offended by this, he cut the tree down. The stump was left, so he was then called 'the Stump Priest'. This made him angrier still, and he dug the stump out, leaving a large hole that filled with water. So then everyone called him 'the Ditch Priest'.

46

In the Yanagihara area there lived an abbot whose nickname was 'the Robbery Priest'. He apparently acquired the name because he was frequently robbed.

47

Someone on a pilgrimage to Kiyomizu Temple[96] fell in with an old nun along the way. As she walked, she repeated over and over: *kusame, kusame*.[97] Why did she keep saying this? he asked. She made no reply, but simply went on muttering the word. Again and again he asked her about it, until she finally lost her temper. 'Oh, for heaven's sake!' she said crossly. 'Look, people say that if this spell isn't spoken when you sneeze, you'll die. Well, I used to be a wet nurse to a boy who's now a young acolyte on Mount Hiei,[98] see, and I'm afraid he may be sneezing at this very moment. That's why I chant.'

What rare devotion!

48

When Count Mitsuchika[99] was in charge of the Sutra Lectures[100] at the palace of Retired Emperor Gotoba, he was summoned to the imperial presence and partook of a meal there. Having finished, he simply pushed the standing tray with its remnants of food out under the nearby screen, and left.[101]

'Good heavens,' the gentlewomen exclaimed to each other, 'how disgusting! Is he expecting us to clean up after him?' But the retired emperor was full of praise for him. 'That was marvellous!' he declared again and again. 'The action of a man deeply versed in courtly precedent.'

49

Do not wait until old age is upon you before taking up religious practice. Most graves of the past hold men who died young.

It may be only when unexpected illness has overtaken you and you are soon to leave this world that you become aware for the first time of past error. By 'error' I mean, quite simply, taking your time over what should be accomplished swiftly, and rushing into what should be dealt with slowly. Regret fills you, but there is no point in repenting now.

You must cling to the certain knowledge that death presses in on us, and never for an instant forget it. If you do this, the corruptions of the world[102] will surely fade from your life, and you will of necessity dedicate yourself in earnest to the Buddhist Way.

In his treatise *The Ten Causes*, Zenrin[103] wrote of a holy man who one day was visited by someone on business that concerned them both. 'There's something urgent I must attend to,' he responded. 'It is almost upon me.' He thereupon blocked his ears, began to recite the *nenbutsu*, and before long was carried into paradise.

The holy man Shinkai[104] was so deeply aware of the transience of this world that he would never relax and sit comfortably, but only ever squatted at the ready.

50

Back in the Ōchō period[105] there was an incident in which a woman who had become a demon was brought up to the capital from Ise. Every day for about twenty days, folk from the capital and nearby Shirakawa[106] came flocking out to have a look at the demon.

Rumours were rife – 'She went to Saionji Temple yesterday'; 'She'll be going to the retired emperor's palace today'; 'She's at Such-and-such right now.' No one claimed to have actually seen her, but no one was prepared to call it all lies either. People from every station in life, high and low, did nothing but talk about the demon.

One day, I was on my way from Higashiyama to the Agui area[107] when I ran into all the folk from north of Shijō, heading north and shouting as they ran, 'The demon's at Ichijō Muromachi!'

I watched from nearby Imade River. The crowd gathered in the area around the imperial viewing stand was so dense that no one could pass. There must be at least some truth in the rumour, I decided, so I sent a fellow to investigate. But it turned out no one had seen the demon. The rowdy mob hung around there until nightfall, and in the end quarrels broke out and some shocking things happened.

Not long after, a two- or three-day illness ran through the populace, and some declared that all the baseless rumours about the demon had been a portent of this.

51

The retired emperor decided to divert water from the Ōi River to flow into the garden pond of his Kameyama Residence,[108] and to this end the local people were ordered to build a water wheel. They were paid extremely well, and spent a number of days at the task – but the wheel completely failed to turn. Various attempts were made to fix it, but to no avail, and in the end it simply stood there, useless.

Then the retired emperor called in villagers from Uji[109] to do the work. They made a wheel with ease and presented it, and it turned just as it should, and drew water wonderfully well.

Whatever the field, experts are a wonderful thing.

52

A monk at Ninnaji Temple had reached old age without ever going to pray at the Iwashimizu Shrine.[110] This saddened him, so one day he decided to go. He set off all alone and on foot, and, having worshipped at Gokurakuji Temple and Kōra Shrine,[111] he went home again, assuming that this was the extent of the pilgrimage site.

To a fellow monk he remarked, 'I've achieved a long-standing ambition. It was a most holy place, and far exceeded all I'd heard of it. But I did wonder why all the pilgrims there went on to climb the mountain. I'd have liked to know what was up there, but I didn't bother going myself, since my aim was to pay my respects to the gods.'

Even in small matters, it's wise to take a guide.

53

Here is another tale of a Ninnaji monk.

A young acolyte was about to become a monk, and everyone got together to say farewell to him with dancing and singing. Drunk and in a fit of high spirits, one fellow seized a three-legged pot[112] that was standing nearby, and pulled it over his head. The thing got stuck halfway, so he pushed down on it till his nose was flattened, then when it covered his face he came prancing out and began to dance, to the great delight of everyone present.

After dancing about for a while, he tried to take the pot off his head, but it wouldn't budge. The jolly atmosphere suddenly palled. No one knew what to do. They tried all manner of things, but after a while his neck began to bleed, and it swelled and swelled until he could scarcely breathe. They next tried to break the pot, but this proved difficult, and the pounding rang in his ears unbearably. This clearly wouldn't work, so there was nothing for it but to drape a gown over the upside-down pot, with the effect that the legs now looked like veiled horns, give the poor man a stick and lead him by the hand to a doctor's house in the city. How people stared as they went past! And how extraordinary he must have looked to the doctor when he was led in and brought before him. His voice was so muffled it was inaudible.

'I've never read of such a case, nor heard of one,' the doctor declared, so the poor fellow went back to Ninnaji. His friends and his old mother gathered around his bed, weeping miserably, but there was no sign that he could hear their sobs.

Eventually, somebody came up with a suggestion. 'Even if his ears and nose come off there's no reason why he should lose his life, after all. Just try pulling as hard as you can.' So they packed protective straw in around the edges, to keep the metal from his neck, and set about pulling. They dragged so hard they almost wrenched his head off, and his ears and nose were gouged right out, but the pot came away. He managed to survive, but he was in a bad way for a long time.

54

There was a beautiful young acolyte in Omuro,[113] and a number of monks set about plotting a way to entice him out to have a good time with them. They enlisted the help of some performing monks[114] and painstakingly made an elegant wooden lidded box, which they carefully placed in a container buried in a handy spot on Narabigaoka Hill.[115] Having scattered fallen leaves over the place so no one would realize anything was there, they went off to the temple and lured the lad out with them.

Delighted, they led him about here and there, then finally they all settled down on a blanket of moss near the buried box.

'My, that was exhausting!'

'Ah, if only someone would "kindle the autumn leaves to warm our wine"!'[116]

'Come on, everyone. See if you can prove those magical powers of yours by producing some miracle[117] with your prayers!'

someone urged, and they turned towards the tree where the box was buried and set about rubbing their rosaries and performing exaggerated *mudras* in an extravagant show of incantation. They then swept aside the leaves – but there was not a thing there.

It must be the wrong place, they decided, and they set about searching the whole mountain, digging everywhere, but they found nothing. Someone had noticed them burying the box, and had stolen it while they went back to the temple. What could they say? They fell into shrill argument, and went home furious.

If you try too hard to be entertaining, it is bound to fall flat.

55

Houses should be built with summer chiefly in mind. One can live anywhere in winter, but a house that is ill suited to hot weather is unbearable.

Deep water is not cooling to the eye. Shallow, running water is far cooler.

A room with a sliding door makes things brighter than one with wooden shutters,[118] and so is better for looking closely at something.

A high ceiling is cold in winter, and darkens the lamplight.

I recall a discussion where all agreed that including areas of no particular use when making a building creates visual interest, and they can be made to serve all sorts of purposes.

56

It is tiresome when someone you meet after long separation regales you with an exhaustive catalogue of all the things that have happened in the meantime. Surely even those who are on close and familiar terms will feel somewhat constrained when they first meet again after some time apart. Unrefined types, on the other hand, will rattle on in breathless excitement about the day's events whenever they return from even a brief outing.

The finer sort of person will direct his story to only one person in a group, and the others are naturally drawn to listen. The lower sort, however, will start talking to no one in particular in the midst of a crowd; he'll paint such vivid descriptions that everyone bursts into raucous laughter, and it's all very rowdy and uncouth. One can judge a man's refinement by whether he restrains his enthusiasm even when talking about interesting things, or laughs a great deal over the most boring story.

If people are discussing the pros and cons of someone's appearance, or a scholar is passing judgement on matters of scholarship, it is most off-putting to hear someone offer himself as a standard of comparison.

57

It is most unfortunate to hear someone relating a tale of the circumstances of some poem,[119] when the poem itself is bad – no one with the slightest understanding of poetry would consider such a poem worthy of discussion.

It is excruciating to listen to anyone holding forth about something they know little about, whatever it may be.

58

'Where you live has no bearing on your dedication to the Way,' some claim. 'What's so difficult about praying for rebirth in paradise while you live in a household and have daily dealings with others?'

Only someone with no understanding of salvation in the next world would say this. If you really do hold this world to be a brief and fleeting place, and dedicate yourself to transcending its suffering, what pleasure could you find in serving your master day in day out, or busying yourself with the concerns of your family? The human heart is easily influenced; without quiet and tranquillity it is hard to pursue a practice of the Way.

These days, people are not made of the stuff of the old ascetics. If they retreat to the wilds of mountain and forest, they nevertheless eat enough to save themselves from starvation, and they cannot get by without some protection from the storms. It is only natural, then, that they should sometimes tend towards worldly desire. But this is absolutely no reason to conclude, 'There's no point in retreating from the world. Just look what happened. Why did he bother even trying?' After all, even if someone who has turned his back on the world and embarked on a practice does still harbour desires, they cannot compare with the lusts of those in powerful places. How much does it cost others to provide him with paper bedding, a hemp robe, a bowl and a meal of rough gruel? Surely his needs are simple, and his heart easily satisfied? For all his occasional urges, shame at his appearance will keep him away from evil temptation and turn him constantly towards good.

The testament to our birth in the human realm should be a strong urge to escape from this world.[120] Surely there can be nothing to distinguish us from the beasts, if we simply devote ourselves to greed and never turn our hearts to the Buddhist Truth.

59

Those who feel the impulse to pursue the path of enlightenment should immediately take the step, and not defer it while they attend to all the other things on their mind. If you say to yourself, 'Let's just wait until after this is over,' or 'While I'm at it I'll just see to that,' or 'People will criticize me about such-and-such so I should make sure it's all dealt with and causes no problem later,' or 'There's been time enough so far, after all, and it won't take long just to a wait a little longer while I do this. Let's not rush into things,' one imperative thing after another will occur to detain you. There will be no end to it all, and the day of decision will never come.

In general, I find that reasonably sensitive and intelligent people will pass their whole life without taking the step they know they should. Would anyone with a fire close behind him choose to pause before fleeing? In a matter of life and death, one casts aside shame, abandons riches and runs. Does mortality wait on our choosing? Death comes upon us more swiftly than fire or flood. There is no escaping it. Who at that moment can refuse to part with all they love – aged parents, beloved children, lord and master, or the love of others?

60

At Shinjōin Temple there once lived a wonderfully learned high-ranking priest named Jōshin,[121] who loved to eat taro roots. He ate them in vast amounts. Even when delivering a sermon, he would always have a dish piled high with taro by his knee, and eat while he read. Whenever he was ill, he would retire to his room for a week or a fortnight 'for treatment', and gorge himself to his heart's content on personally chosen taro of the finest quality. This is how he cured every illness. He never gave any to anyone else to eat. He ate them all himself.

Jōshin was extremely poor, but his teacher on his deathbed bequeathed to him the sum of two hundred *kan*[122] plus monks' living quarters. He sold the building for one hundred *kan*, and dedicated the combined sum of 30,000 *hiki* to the purchase of taro. He gave this money to an acquaintance in the city for safekeeping, and drew out ten *kan* at a time to keep himself well supplied with taro. This was all he used the money for, and eventually it was all gone. 'What extraordinary piety,' everyone said, 'to come by three hundred *kan* when he was so poor, and choose to use it like this.'

Jōshin once gave the nickname 'Shiroururi'[123] to a monk he saw. 'What does that mean?' everyone asked, to which he replied, 'I've no idea. But if such a thing existed, I believe it would look like this fellow's face.'

Jōshin was not only handsome but physically strong, a great eater, and excelled in calligraphy, scholarship and oratory. He was a leading light in the sect, and was of course valued highly in his own temple as well. However, he was an eccentric who placed little value on the world, went his own way in all things and never deferred to others.

At banquets after mass sutra readings,[124] he wouldn't wait for all the others to be served but set in to eat as soon as his own meal was before him; then, when he wanted to leave, he simply got to his feet by himself and went off. He never ate at the prescribed times[125] like everyone else, but whenever he wanted, be it the middle of the night or at dawn; if he felt sleepy he would retire to bed whatever the time of day, and pay no attention to others' entreaties no matter how important the occasion. Once awake, however, he would stay up without sleep for nights on end, wandering serenely about humming to himself. Yet for all his extraordinary ways he wasn't disliked, and was given free rein to do as he wanted. It must have been on account of his great virtue.

61

There is no official sanction for the practice of dropping a rice steamer from the roof when an imperial child is born.[126] It is a form of magic to ensure easy delivery of the afterbirth. If things are going well, it is not done. The practice originated among the lower orders, and has no particular foundation. A steamer from the village of Ōhara[127] is traditionally used. There is a picture in an old treasure house of a steamer being dropped during the birth of a commoner's child.

62

When Enseimon-in[128] was a little girl, she asked someone who was visiting her father, the retired emperor, to deliver this poem to him:

With the letter that reads 'two'	*futatsu moji*
and with an ox's horns	*ushi no tsuno moji*
with the straight one	*sugu na moji*
and with the crooked one –	*yugami moji to zo*
so do I yearn for you.[129]	*kimi wa oboyuru*

The meaning is that she yearned for him 'lovingly'.

63

The officiating holy priest at the Goshichinichi service[130] brings in armed strongmen to act as guards, a pretentious gesture that grew out of an occasion when robbers once broke in. Since the coming year is presaged by how smoothly things go during these ceremonies, the use of soldiers is unsettling.

64

Someone in a position to know once pointed out that the use of an ox carriage with five-corded screens[131] is not necessarily a matter of rank alone. They may be used once one has attained the highest rank and position that one's birth permits.

65

These days, the formal lacquered cap[132] of the court is far higher than it used to be. Those who still use an old-fashioned hat box add an extra section, to fit it in.

66

The Okamoto Chancellor[133] once instructed the Imperial Falconer, Shimotsuke no Takekatsu, to present a brace of pheasants for the table attached to a bough of red plum in full bloom. Takekatsu replied that he knew nothing of the art of attaching birds to flowering boughs, let alone how he should attach two birds. The chancellor asked the head chef as well as various others, and at length came back and told him that he should attach the birds for presentation in any way he chose. So Takekatsu presented one pheasant, attached to a plum bough without flowers.

Takekatsu explained that when a bird is to be presented attached to a bough, the plum branch should be either in bud or with petals falling. One may also use a bough of white pine. The bough should be six or seven feet long, severed with two opposing diagonal cuts, the second being roughly half an inch deep.[134] The bird is attached to the centre of a forked bough, with the body tied to one branch and the feet resting on the other. It should be bound in two places with an unsplit cord of wisteria vine. One cuts the ends of the vine to match the length of the wing-base feathers, and bends them in the shape of ox's horns. On the morning of the year's first snowfall, take the bough on your shoulder and carry it in through the central gate, walking in the prescribed manner.[135] Follow the paving stones under the eaves, taking care not to mark the snow. Lightly scatter a little fine down from the haunches, and prop the bough against the railing of the wing building.[136] If you receive a gift of clothing, put it over your shoulder, perform the gestures of thanks[137] and retreat. Though it should be first snowfall, the pheasant is not presented unless the snow is high enough to cover the tips of the shoes. No doubt the down is scattered because it is at the downy base of the thighs that the hawk seizes the pheasant, he added.

Why is it that a bird is not attached to a flowering bough? In *The Tales of Ise* we read of a pheasant attached to an artificial bough of plum during the ninth month, with the poem 'These flowers I pluck for you, my lord / know nothing of time.'[138] Perhaps, then, artificial flowers are permitted.

67

The respective deities of the Iwamoto and Hashimoto subshrines within the Kamo Shrine[139] are the poets Narihira and Sanekata.[140] People are always confusing the two, so one year when I visited the Kamo Shrine I called over an old shrine priest who was passing and asked him about it.

'I believe the shrine was dedicated to Sanekata because his reflection fell in the waters of the sacred stream, so since the stream flows close by the Hashimoto Shrine, that would be his,' he told me. 'I have heard that Abbot Yoshimizu's poem[141]

That genteel man	*tsuki wo mede*
who once in bygone days	*hana wo nagameshi*
sang the moon's praises	*inishie no*
and gazed upon the blossoms – *he*	*yasashiki hito wa*
now is *here*	*koko ni ariwara*

refers to the Iwamoto Shrine. But you will know far more of this than I, I'm sure.' He explained it all most courteously, and I was deeply impressed.

When she was young, Lady Konoe,[142] who had a great many poems chosen for inclusion in the Collections, used often to compose a hundred-poem sequence which she then wrote in ink she made using sacred water from the stream before these two shrines, and dedicated to them. She had a very fine reputation, and people recited many of her poems. She was also an excellent writer of Chinese poetry and its prefaces.

68

There was once a certain constable of some sort in Tsukushi[143] who believed that the white radish was a wonderful remedy for all ills. Every morning for many years, he would roast two and eat them.

One day, his enemies seized a moment when the house was for once unguarded and empty to raid the place. They surrounded the house and attacked, whereupon two warriors emerged from the building and fought them back with no thought for their own lives, sending them all fleeing.

The constable was mystified. 'Why should men who have no apparent connection to the place such as yourselves fight for it in this manner?' he asked. 'Who are you?'

'We are the two white radishes that you put such faith in and eat every morning,' they replied, and then they vanished.

Clearly, his deep faith had produced this fine reward.

69

The holy man of Shosha[144] had accumulated such merit through recitations of *The Lotus Sutra* that he had attained purity of the Six Senses.[145]

Once, on a journey, he entered the lodging where he was to stay the night and heard the bubbling of a pot of beans being boiled over a fire made from their husks. 'We're so closely related and yet you boil us so brutally!' they were crying, and the bean husks crackling in the flames seemed to him to reply, 'Do you imagine we're boiling you on purpose? It's excruciating for us to be burning like this, heaven knows, but we're powerless to stop. Enough of these recriminations!'

70

During the Gen'ō era, the precious *biwa* named 'Gyoyū' went missing, and at the imperial music performance in the Seishodō[146] the Kikutei Minister[147] instead played the 'Bokuba'.

Once seated, he immediately tested the frets, and one of them promptly fell off. He stuck it back on with some rice glue he was carrying tucked into the fold of his robe, and by the time the offerings had been made at the altar it had dried in place, and all was well. A woman from the audience dressed in travelling robes, who must have had some grudge against him, had apparently gone over and pulled off the fret, then replaced it as before.

71

As soon as I hear someone's name, I feel I can picture their face, but when I actually meet them no one ever looks as I had been imagining all that time.

Also, I wonder if everyone, on hearing some old tale, imagines it as taking place in a certain part of some house he knows, and identifies the characters with people he sees in life, as I do.

And is it just I who sometimes feels a conviction that what someone is saying, or what you're seeing or thinking just then, has already happened before, though you cannot remember when?

72

Unpleasant things – a great many things cluttering up the area where someone is sitting. A lot of brushes lying on an ink stone. A crowd of Buddhist images in a private worship hall.[148] A large collection of stones and plants in a garden. Too many children and grandchildren in a house. Too much talk when meeting others. A long list of one's virtuous acts in a supplicatory prayer.[149]

Things that are not unpleasant in large amounts are books on a book cart, and rubbish on a rubbish heap.

73

Stories that get passed around are for the most part lies, no doubt because the truth is so boring. People will exaggerate the facts in their telling, and with the distance of time and place they will feel increasingly free to tell a story in any way they choose; then it gets written down, and this becomes the received version.

The impressive feats of someone skilled in one of the arts will be reported as nothing short of miraculous by ignorant fools who know nothing of the art in question, while those who do know won't believe a word of it. Things witnessed are never the same as the rumour of them.

If the speaker lets his words run away with him without bothering to disguise their falsehood, his listeners will soon realize there is no truth in what he says. If someone repeats a story he himself guesses is untrue, nose twitching in self-satisfied pleasure, it is not his own lie he is telling but another's. More alarming is a fabrication told by someone quite convincingly, with a few of the details plausibly blurred, hinting that he's not quite sure of all the facts, yet in a way that makes perfect sense of the story.

People will not take much issue with an invented tale if it shows them in a good light.

When everyone is enjoying someone's free embellishment of a story, you can't very well be the only one who points out that that wasn't actually how it happened, and as you listen you may even find yourself drawn in as confirming witness, and end up helping to establish this version as fact.

Yes, one way and another, this world is full of lies. The only safe approach is to treat everything you hear as completely normal and unremarkable.

The tales told by common folk are simply astonishing to hear. People of refinement never tell tales of the strange and marvellous. Nevertheless, this does not mean one should necessarily disbelieve the stories of the miraculous powers of the gods and buddhas, or legends of their manifesting in earthly form. It is foolish to be credulous of all the tall tales people tell about such things, but there is no point in doubting everything you hear either. As a rule, you should accept such stories at face value, neither believing everything nor ridiculing it all as nonsense.

74

We swarm like ants, scurrying to east and west, dashing to north and south, folk of high birth and of low, old and young, some going, others returning, sleeping at night, rising again next morning . . . What is all this busyness? There is no end to our greed for life, our lust for gain.

We tend our bodies – to what end? Old age and death are the only sure things awaiting us. Swiftly they come, without an instant's pause. What pleasure is to be found while we await them?

The deluded have no fear of this truth. In thrall to the lure of fame and fortune, they never pause to see what lies so close before them. Fools mourn it. In their longing for eternal life, they have no understanding of the law of mutability.

75

What kind of man will feel depressed at being idle? There is nothing finer than to be alone with nothing to distract you.

If you follow the ways of the world, your heart will be drawn to its sensual defilements and easily led astray; if you go among people, your words will be guided by others' responses rather than come from the heart. There is nothing firm or stable in a life spent between larking about together and quarrelling, exuberant one moment, aggrieved and resentful the next. You are forever pondering pros and cons, endlessly absorbed in questions of gain and loss. And on top of delusion comes drunkenness, and in that drunkenness you dream.

Scurrying and bustling, heedless and forgetful – such are all men. Even if you do not yet understand the True Way, you can achieve what could be termed temporary happiness at least by removing yourself from outside influences, taking no part in the affairs of the world, calming yourself and stilling the mind. As

The Great Cessation and Insight[150] says, we must 'break all ties with everyday life, human affairs, the arts and scholarship'.

76

When guests are thronging to pay their respects to some highly acclaimed family on a joyous or sorrowful occasion, wandering monks really should not be seen hanging around, mingling with the crowd and ingratiating themselves.

Even if they have some reason for being there, monks should stay aloof from others.

77

I cannot bear the way people will make it their business to know all the details of some current rumour, even though it has nothing to do with them, and then proceed to pass the story on and do their best to learn more. Wandering monks up from some provincial backwater seem particularly adept at prying into tales about others as if it was their own concern, and spreading the word in such detail that you wonder how on earth they came to know so much.

78

Nor can I bear the way people will spread excited rumours about the latest marvels. A refined person will not learn of things until the rumours are old and stale.

If someone new comes visiting, the boorish and insensitive will always manage to make the visitor feel ignorant by exchanging cryptic remarks about something they all know among themselves, some story or name, chuckling and exchanging knowing glances.

79

It is best not to seem too deeply acquainted with any subject.

Do we find people of refinement proudly holding forth on

some topic, just because they happen to know about it? Some provincial boor, on the other hand, will assure you that he knows all about anything you happen to ask. Sometimes a man can genuinely impress you with how well informed he is, but on the whole such people appear stupidly complacent and self-satisfied.

It is truly impressive to speak only reluctantly about something you thoroughly understand, and not to mention it at all unless asked.

80

People seem to be drawn to pursue precisely those things that are quite unrelated to their normal life.

A monk will practise the arts of the warrior, while uncouth soldiers from the eastern provinces disdain to study archery and instead pretend to know all about the Buddhist Law, or delight in composing linked verse or making music together. Yet they are even more despised for this than for the second-rate performance of their own profession.

Not only monks, but a great many men of even the highest ranks, court nobles and senior courtiers, are fond of the military arts. In fact, however, you may fight a hundred battles and win them all but it still won't assure you fame as a warrior. Anyone can look the part of warrior when luck allows him to overthrow his opponent. It is only when you have run through every weapon, your last arrow is shot, and you accept death without surrendering that you have truly gained such a name. While you still live, you have no cause to boast of your prowess.

The way of the warrior is closer to the behaviour of beasts than of virtuous men; its cultivation is pointless unless you are born of warrior stock.

81

Crude brushwork in the pictures and writing on standing screens and sliding doors is not so much ugly in its own right as an indication of the poor taste of the owner.

Very often, there will be pieces of furniture in a house that disappoint with their crassness. Not that one should always have excellent furniture, of course; I speak here of items where the desire to protect from damage results in tasteless and unattractive work, or those that have unnecessary bits added to them or strive for effect in order to make them interesting.

The best things are those that have a somewhat antique air, are unpretentious and are inexpensive but well made.

82

When someone complained that it was a great shame the way fine silk covers[151] are so soon damaged, Ton'a[152] replied, 'It is only after the top and bottom edges of the silk have frayed, or when the mother-of-pearl has peeled off the roller, that a scroll is truly impressive' – an astonishingly fine remark, I felt. Similarly, an unmatched set of bound books can be considered unattractive, but Bishop Kōyū[153] impressed me deeply by saying that only a boring man will always want things to match; real quality lies in irregularity – another excellent remark.

In all things, perfect regularity is tasteless. Something left not quite finished is very appealing, a gesture towards the future. Someone told me that even in the construction of the imperial palace, some part is always left uncompleted.

In the Buddhist scriptures and other works written by the great men of old there are also a number of missing sections.

83

The Chikurin'in Novice and Minister of the Left[154] was set to advance smoothly to Chief Minister, yet he took the tonsure before promotion, declaring that he would retire while still minister since his future prospects bored him. Later, the Tōin Minister of the Left[155] was very much in sympathy with this; he too was without any ambition to advance to the highest post.

'The dragon that has scaled the heights laments his coming fall,' as the saying goes. The moon swells to the full only to wane; things first prosper and then decay. It is the way of things that whatever has reached its apogee must thereafter decline.

84

The Chinese divine Fa Xian,[156] when he went to India, wept at the sight of a fan from his native land, and when he was ill requested Chinese food. On hearing of this, someone said, 'To think that a great man like him should reveal such weakness to those in a foreign land.' But Bishop Kōyū exclaimed, 'Such fine depth of feeling!' – a wonderfully genteel response, I thought, and quite un-priest-like.

85

No human heart is quite guileless; there is some deceit in all. But why should there not be the occasional person who is honest and upright?

One may not be without guile oneself, but it is human nature to envy others who are wise and good. Really stupid people who come across the rare wise man, however, will hate him. 'He turns up his nose at small gains because in his heart he hopes for bigger ones,' they sneer. 'It's all a hypocritical pose, intended to impress and make a name for himself.'

Such a man scoffs so contemptuously because the other's nature differs from his own, but this only reveals what he himself is like – a born fool, who has no hope of transcending his own nature. Even the pretence of turning down a chance of some small gain would be beyond him; likewise the merest imitation of wisdom.

If you run about the streets pretending to be a madman, then a madman is what you are. If in pretence of being wicked you kill a man, wicked is what you are. A horse that pretends to fleetness must be counted among the fleet; a man who models himself on the saintly Emperor Shun[157] will indeed be among his number. Even a deceitful imitation of wisdom will place you among the wise.

86

Counsellor Koretsugu[158] has a wealth of literary talent. He has spent his life in austerities and devoted chanting of the sutras.

He was lodging at Miidera Temple with Abbot En'i when the complex was razed in the fire of the Bunpō era,[159] and when they met afterwards he said, 'I have always referred to you by the common term "Temple Priest", but now you will be simply Priest, minus temple.' This was a very clever thing to say.[160]

87

One should be careful in giving the lower orders alcohol.

A man from Uji was on close terms with a monk of great refinement in the capital by the name of Gukaku,[161] who was his wife's brother. One day, he sent a servant with a horse to bring Gukaku to Uji.

'It's a long journey,' Gukaku remarked. 'I'll just give the fellow a drink before we set off.' He produced some sake, and the servant proceeded to toss back cup after cup.

He was a fine, dependable-looking fellow with a sword hanging from his belt, so Gukaku felt quite safe in his care. Off they set together, but when they reached Kohata they came across some Nara monks,[162] accompanied by a large band of warriors. The servant drew himself up and confronted them: 'Halt! Why are you lurking about in the mountains so suspiciously after dark?' He drew his sword, and his opponents likewise drew theirs, and slotted arrows to bows.

Seeing this preparation for battle, Gukaku rubbed his hands together beseechingly and began to plead. 'He's out of his mind with drink!' he cried. 'Do forgive him, I beg you!' At this, they all jeered and went on their way.

The servant turned angrily on Gukaku. 'What a thing to do! I'm not drunk! I was about to perform a fine feat in your service, and now this sword is quite useless thanks to you,' and so saying he slashed wildly at Gukaku till he tumbled from his horse.

'Help! Bandits!' he then cried, and when a posse of local villagers appeared in response the servant rushed after them, laying about him with his sword and yelling, 'I'm the bandit!' till the gang of villagers together managed to overcome him, throw him to the ground and tie him up.

Gukaku's horse galloped off down the Uji road, and when it arrived home, covered in blood, its horrified master sent a large group of men running to investigate. They found Gukaku lying groaning in a field of gardenia bushes, and carried him back.

Gukaku managed to escape with his life, but he sustained wounds to his back that left him a cripple.

88

A man claimed that the copy of the *Wakan rōeishū*[163] in his collection was made by the famous calligrapher Ono no Tōfū.[164]

'I wouldn't wish to suggest that family tradition was unfounded of course,' someone said to him, 'but surely Tōfū lived at a different time from the compiler of this work, the Shijō Grand Counsellor? There's something odd here.'

But at this the owner of the book only treasured it the more, on the grounds that in that case it was even more rare and precious.

89

Someone claimed that deep in the mountains there lived a man-eating beast called the *nekomata*. 'It's not just in the mountains,' someone else said. 'It's said around here too that once a cat has reached a grand old age it turns into a *nekomata* and will eat people.'

This was overheard by a certain Amidabutsu, a monk who lived near Gyōganji and composed linked verse.[165] 'People like me who go out alone need to be careful,' he thought to himself.

Around this time, he happened to stay out till late at a linked verse gathering. He was on his was home by himself when, on the bank of the Kogawa, he suddenly spied heading straight for him a *nekomata* such as he'd been hearing of, which leaped at him and made to bite him in the neck. Overcome with terror, the monk hadn't the strength to try to defend himself; his legs gave under him, and he tumbled into the stream. 'Help! *Nekomata! Nekomata!*' he yelled.

People rushed out from the nearby houses with lighted torches, and recognized the familiar figure of the monk. 'What happened?' they asked as they helped him out of the water. Tucked into his bosom were the prizes he'd won in the linked verse competition that evening, a scroll and a small box, now thoroughly sodden. Off he crawled back home, with the air of one who had barely escaped with his life.

Apparently it was his own dog, which had recognized its master in the dark, rushed over and leaped up to greet him.

90

The Dainagon Abbot employed a young acolyte by the name of Otozuru-maru, who came to be on intimate terms with one Yasura-dono[166] and was constantly coming and going to visit him.

One day, seeing the lad return, the abbot asked where he had been. 'I've been to see Yasura-dono,' he replied.

'Is this Yasura-dono a layman, or a monk?' enquired the abbot.

Bringing his sleeves together in a polite bow, the acolyte replied, 'I really don't know, sir. I've never seen his head.'[167]

I wonder why not – after all, he would have seen the rest of him.

91

The Yin-Yang masters[168] do not concern themselves with those days of the calendar marked 'Red Tongue Days'.[169] Nor did people of old treat the day as unpropitious. It seems someone more recently has declared it unlucky, and now everyone has begun to avoid it, believing that things undertaken on this day will miscarry. This idea – that whatever is said or done on this day will fail, that objects gained on the day will be lost and plans made will go awry – is ridiculous. If you count the number of failures that happen on an auspicious day, you will find there are just as many.

This is because, in this transient phenomenal world with its constant change, what appears to exist in fact does not. What is begun has no end. Aims go unfulfilled, yet desire is endless. The human heart changes ceaselessly. All things are passing illusion. What is there that remains unchanging? The folly of such beliefs springs from people's inability to understand this.

It is said that evil performed on an auspicious day is always ill-fated, while good performed on an inauspicious one will be blessed by good fortune. It is people who create good fortune and misfortune, not the calendar.

92

A man who was studying archery took two arrows in his hand[170] and stood before the target.

'A beginner should not hold two arrows,' his teacher told him. 'You will be careless with the first, knowing you have a second. You must always be determined to hit the target with the single arrow you shoot, and have no thought beyond this.' With only two arrows, and standing before his master, would he really be inclined to be slapdash with one of them? Yet although he may not have been aware of his own carelessness, his teacher was. The same injunction surely applies in all matters.

A man engaged in Buddhist practice will tell himself at night that there is always the morning, or in the morning will anticipate the night, always intending to make more effort later. And if such are your days, how much less aware must you be of the passing moment's indolence. Why should it be so difficult to carry something out right now when you think of it, to seize the instant?

93

Someone told the following tale. A man sells an ox. The buyer says he will come in the morning to pay and take the beast. But during the night, the ox dies. 'The buyer thus gained, while the seller lost,' he concluded.

But a bystander remarked, 'The owner did indeed lose on the transaction, but he profited greatly in another way. Let me tell you why. Living creatures have no knowledge of the nearness of death. Such was the ox, and such too are we humans. As it happened, the ox died that night; as it happened, the owner lived on. One day's life is more precious than a fortune's worth of money, while an ox's worth weighs no more than a goose feather. One cannot say that a man who gains a fortune while losing a coin or two has made a loss.'

Everyone laughed at this. 'That reasoning doesn't only apply to the owner of the ox,' they scoffed.

The man went on. 'Well then, if people hate death they should love life. Should we not relish each day the joy of survival? Fools forget this – they go striving after other enjoyments, cease to appreciate the fortune they have and risk all to lay their hands on fresh wealth. Their desires are never sated. There is a deep contradiction in failing to enjoy life and yet fearing death when faced with it. It is because they have no fear of death that people fail to enjoy life – no, not that they don't fear it, but rather they forget its nearness. Of course, it must be said that the ultimate gain lies in transcending the relative world with its distinction between life and death.'

At this, everyone jeered more than ever.

94

The Tokiwai Chief Minister[171] was on his way to his duties at the palace one day when he met an imperial guard who had come with a message from the emperor. The man dismounted from his horse to present it. Later, the Chief Minister remarked to His Majesty that a certain guard of his had dismounted while holding an imperial message. 'How can such a fellow be in your service?' he said. The man was relieved of his position.

One must proffer an imperial message from horseback, not dismount.

95

I once asked someone familiar with court customs and precedents on which side the ring for the cord should be attached on a lacquered box.[172] 'There are two theories,' he replied. 'One says it should go on the "roller" or left side, the other that it should be on the "cover" or right.[173] Both are permissible. Most document boxes have it on the right. Boxes for sundries usually place it on the left.'

96

There is a plant called *menamomi*.[174] When someone is bitten by a viper, he will quickly recover if he crushes the leaf and applies it to the bite. One should learn to recognize it.

97

There are endless examples of something that attaches itself to another, eats away at it and harms it. A body has fleas. A house has rats. A nation has robbers. A lesser man has wealth. An honourable man has moral imperatives.[175] A monk has the Buddhist Law.

98

Here are some things that particularly spoke to me among the teachings I read in a book called *Superb Small Sermons*[176] or something of the sort, a collection of the teachings of venerable holy men:

– When hesitating between doing and not doing something, it is generally better not to do it.

– One with his thoughts fixed on the world to come should not own so much as a pickling jar.[177] Even the possession of a fine copy of the sutras or a nicely made Buddhist image[178] is wrong.

– The highest way of living for those who take the tonsure is to aim to lack nothing while owning nothing.

– Monks of high degree should become as lowly monks, a wise man should become foolish, a wealthy man poor, a skilled man talentless.

– If you wish to follow the Buddhist Way, you should simply retire and make time in your life, and not let your mind dwell on worldly matters. This is the most important thing.

I have forgotten the others.

99

The Horikawa Chief Minister[179] was a handsome and wealthy man, who loved luxury in all things.

He appointed his son Lord Mototoshi[180] as Director of Police and, when his son took over the position, declared the document box in his office to be ugly, and ordered it to be refashioned into something more impressive. Officials conversant with the old customs, however, pointed out that the box had been inherited down the ages; no one knew its date, but it was several hundred years old. An object such as this, which had been in official use for generations, was prized as a model precisely because it was so old and dilapidated, they said, so there were grave difficulties with the idea of refashioning it.

Hearing this, the Minister changed his mind.

100

The Koga Chief Minister wished to drink some water one day when he was in the Privy Chamber,[181] and one of the groundskeepers offered it to him in an earthenware cup. 'Bring a wooden vessel,'[182] he ordered, and this is what he drank from.

101

Once, the man who was chief administrator of the ministerial investiture ceremony at the time mistakenly proceeded to the ceremonial venue without receiving the necessary imperial edict from the Compiler of Documents. This was a most appalling blunder, but it was impossible to go back and get it.

He couldn't think what to do, but the sixth-rank Conveyor of Documents Yasutsuna[183] appealed to a gentlewoman dressed in travelling robes and had her fetch the imperial edict, which she surreptitiously passed to the chief administrator – a wonderfully clever thing to do.

102

When the Grand Counsellor Count Mitsutada[184] was in charge of the Great Demon Expulsion ceremony, he asked for procedural guidance from the Tōin Minister of the Right.[185] 'The wisest course is to take that fellow Matagorō[186] as your teacher,' the minister told him.

This Matagorō was an old retainer in the guards who was well versed in court ritual. On one delightful occasion, the Konoe Minister[187] summoned the Conveyor of Documents as soon as he had seated himself for a ceremony, having forgotten that the kneeling mat should be in place, and Matagorō, who was attending to the fires nearby, murmured softly, 'I believe the kneeling mat should be placed first.'

103

Once the retired emperor's close retainers at the Daikakuji Palace[188] were playing at making and solving riddles, when the physician Tadamori[189] happened along.

Advisor and Grand Counsellor Lord Kin'akira[190] proposed the following riddle: 'What would you call a foreign-looking "Tadamori"?'

'*Kara-heiji* – a Chinese sake flask!'[191] someone cried, and they all burst into laughter, whereupon Tadamori walked out in high dudgeon.

104

A lady who had reason to withdraw from the world for a time had retired to a lonely tumbledown house, where she was idling away the long days of her seclusion, when one dimly moonlit evening a certain man decided to call; but as he was creeping stealthily to her door, a dog set up a fierce barking. This brought one of the maidservants. 'Where do you hail from?' she enquired. The man promptly announced himself, and was shown in.

His heart was heavy as he took in his forlorn surroundings. How must she spend her time here? He stood hesitating on the veranda's rough wooden boards. 'This way,' came a wonderfully serene and youthful voice, so he slid open the door with some difficulty and entered.

The place was not so shabby after all, but was modest and refined. At the far end a lamp shone softly, revealing the beauty of the furnishings, and the scent of incense lit some time earlier imbued the place with an evocative and beguiling air.

He heard orders being given among the servants – 'Take care to lock the gate. It may rain. Put the carriage under the shelter of the gate roof' – and talk of where his retainers should spend the night. Then one added, in a soft murmur that nevertheless reached his ears because he was quite close, 'Tonight at least we can sleep easy.'

The two spoke together of all that had happened since they last met, until the first cock crowed while it was yet night. On they talked earnestly, of matters past and to come, and now the cock's crow was loud and persistent. The day must by now have dawned, he thought, but this was not a place he must hasten to leave before light, so he lingered on a little, until sunlight whitened the cracks in the door. At last, with promises not to forget her, he departed.

Recalling the enchanting scene, he remembers how beautifully green the trees and garden plants glowed in that early summer daybreak, and even now, whenever he passes the house, he turns to gaze until the great camphor tree in the garden is lost to sight.

105

The snow drifts lie still deeply frozen in the shade to the house's north, and frost glitters on the shafts of the carriage drawn up there; the dawn moon shines clear yet subtly touched with shadow, and there on the edge of the gallery of the little worship hall,[192] tucked away from the world, sit a man and a woman, evidently distinguished people, deep in some apparently endless conversation. Her head, her features – all is wonderfully elegant, and there comes a delightful sudden whiff of an indescribable fragrance. One is intrigued, too, by the occasional snatches of conversation that come drifting over.

106

Shōkū, a holy man from the great monastery on Mount Kōya,[193] was on his way to the capital one day when, on a narrow path, he met coming the other way a horse ridden by a woman and led by a servant. The man tugged the horse past him so clumsily that Shōkū and his horse were pushed into the ditch.

Incensed, Shōkū berated the fellow. 'What extraordinary rudeness! I'll have you know that of the four categories of the Buddha's followers the nun is below the monk, the novice below the nun and the novice nun below the novice monk. It's an unheard-of violation for a novice nun to push a monk into a ditch!'

'What are you talking about? I can't understand a word you're saying,' the fellow replied.

Shōkū gasped with rage. 'How dare you, you irreligious ignoramus!' he spat, then, obviously satisfied that he had thoroughly had his say, he turned his horse and beat a retreat the way he had come.

A most pious altercation!

107

In the days of Retired Emperor Kameyama,[194] some mischievous gentlewomen at court decided that, since it was so unusual to find a man who could produce an impressive off-the-cuff response to something a lady had said, they would have some fun testing each young man who came to visit by asking whether he had heard the *hototogisu* sing yet,[195] to see if it would elicit a sensitive reply.

A certain Grand Counsellor's response was, 'A man of no account such as myself has not the ears to hear it.'[196]

'I believe I heard one at Iwakura,' was the Horikawa Palace Minister's[197] reply.

'This is an acceptable response,' the ladies decided. ' "A man of no account such as myself" is pretentious.'

A man should be brought up so as to avoid being the butt of women's laughter. Someone once remarked that the Jōdoji Chancellor[198] spoke so beautifully because hé was well instructed by the former empress Ankimon'in[199] as a child. The Yamashina Minister of the Left[200] once remarked that even to have the eyes of a lowly serving girl on him made him feel horribly awkward and self-conscious. If there were no women in this world, surely no one would bother over the niceties of how one should wear one's clothing or lacquered cap.

So just how splendid are these women who provoke such humiliations in a man? Well, in fact, all women are by nature perverse. Deeply self-centred, thoroughly avaricious, unreasoning, their hearts can slip in an instant into error. They are clever with words, but will refuse to answer when asked something quite innocuous – yet where you imagine they would be carefully discreet, they will come out with astonishing revelations quite unsolicited. You would think they were even more adept than men at calculating and dissembling, but they're quite unconcerned by being later shown up.

It is the way of women to be devious and foolish. How pitiful we men are, to submit ourselves to such creatures and attempt to impress them. Why, after all, should we feel so awkward in their presence?

If such a thing as a wise woman did exist, we would no doubt find her quite unapproachable and off-putting. Only a man who is led astray and mastered by a woman's charms will see her as tender and delightful.

108

No one begrudges the passing moment. Is this because they are wise, or because they are fools? To the lazy fools among them

I would say: a single coin may be next to worthless, but it is through their accumulation that the poor man becomes rich. This is why the merchant is so keen to save every coin he can. You may not be aware of the moments, but as long as they continue to pass, you will very soon find yourself at the end of life. Thus, one dedicated to the Way must not concern himself over the distant future. His only care should be not to let the present moment slip vainly through his fingers.

Imagine someone comes to you and announces that you will die tomorrow. How will you spend your last day? What entertainment could you find?[201] How would you busy yourself? And how is this day we are now living different from that final day?

We inevitably waste most of each day in eating and drinking, defecating, sleeping, talking and walking about. For the tiny remainder of our time, we do worthless things, speak worthless words, think worthless thoughts. And not only do we pass the moments in this way, but whole days, whole months pass thus – a lifetime. This is supreme folly.

Xie Lingyun[202] was recorder of the translation of *The Lotus Sutra*, but he was taken up with thoughts of his own advancement, so Hui Yuan refused to include him in his pious Bailian group.[203]

Lose for a moment your grasp of the passing instant and you are as good as dead. You ask why time should be so precious? It is so that you may concentrate the mind on banishing all idle thoughts, refrain from engaging in worldly matters and meditate if this is what you choose, or perform austerities if that is your chosen path.

109

A man famed for his tree-climbing skills once directed another to climb a tall tree and cut branches. While the fellow was precariously balanced aloft, the tree-climber watched without a word, but when he was descending and had reached the height of the eaves the expert called to him, 'Careful how you go! Take care coming down!'

'Why do you say that? He's so far down now that he could leap to the ground from there,' I said.

'Just so,' replied the tree-climber. 'While he's up there among the treacherous branches I need not say a word – his fear is enough to guide him. It's in the easy places that mistakes will always occur.'

Lowly commoner though he was, his words echoed the warnings of the sages.

Apparently one of the laws of kickball[204] also states that if you relax after achieving a difficult kick, this is the moment when the ball will always fall to the ground.

110

I once asked someone skilled at the board game of *sugoroku*[205] for hints on how to play. 'Don't play to win,' he said. 'Play not to lose. Consider what moves would make you lose most quickly, and avoid them. Choose a method that will make you lose after your opponent, even if only by a single square.'

This lesson from one who knows his art equally applies to the arts of governing both self and nation.

111

I still remember with awe hearing a holy man declare that in his opinion those who devote themselves day in day out to playing *go*[206] or *sugoroku* are committing a sin more heinous than the Four Transgressions or the Five Wickednesses.[207]

112

No one, hearing that someone is setting out the next day on a long journey, will confront them with something to attend to that requires their calm and undivided attention. A man in the midst of a sudden major upheaval or terrible sorrow is in no position to listen to talk about other matters, or to enquire about the griefs and joys of others. No one would think to complain of his remissness. And the same applies, surely, to those of advancing years or visited by illness, not to mention those who have chosen to leave the world for a life of religious devotion.

None of the requirements of human interaction and etiquette can be easily avoided. If we insist on being punctilious in all those worldly demands so difficult to ignore, it will only add to desires, shackle our lives and leave no space in our hearts for calm detachment, and we will end up wasting our entire life being driven to distraction by trivial matters.

'Night closes in, the way is long. / My feet have stumbled on life's road.'[208] Now is the time to cast off all worldly ties. Turn your back on loyalty. Think no more of propriety. Those who fail to understand are free to call you mad, deranged, lacking all feeling. No censure can hurt you now, nor praise sway you.

113

It cannot be helped if a man over forty secretly indulges in love affairs, but it is disgusting and unseemly for him to openly discuss such matters, or gossip and joke about sexual matters or other people's personal lives.

It is generally quite repellent when old men mingle with the young and try to impress them with their talk, or to witness a man of no consequence speaking casually of some well-known person as if they were on intimate terms, or an impoverished man who loves throwing parties and puts on grand displays to entertain the guests.

114

When the Imadegawa Minister[209] arrived at the ford across the Arisu River on his way to Saga one day in an ox-drawn carriage, his driver Saiōmaru pushed the beast across so fast that water came splashing up on to the front board of the carriage.

'Idiot fellow!' exclaimed Tamenori,[210] who was seated in the rear. 'What a place to urge an ox like that!'

The Minister was furious. 'Do you claim to know better than Saiōmaru how to drive an ox? You're the idiot!' and he struck Tamenori's head against the side of the carriage.

This famous Saiōmaru was employed by the Uzumasa lord,[211] and was ox driver to the emperor. The gentlewomen in service to the Uzumasa lord were given interesting names[212] – one was Hisasachi, another Kototsuchi, another Hōhara, and there was also Otoushi.

115

A large group of *boro* priests[213] had gathered at a place called Shukugahara[214] and were chanting the Nine Nenbutsus,[215] when another from elsewhere arrived, and asked if there was a monk by the name of Irowoshi among them.

'I am Irowoshi,' came a voice from their midst. 'Who speaks?'

'My name is Shirabonji. I've heard that my teacher' – he gave a name – 'was killed by a *boro* named Irowoshi up in the eastern provinces. I ask because I'm hoping to meet this man and repay the grudge I owe him.'

'Bravely spoken! It happened as you describe. If we face off here, we will desecrate holy ground. Let's fight it out on the riverbank over there. Please don't come to the aid of either of us, my friends. If too many people get caught up in this it will interfere with the rituals.'

Having agreed on this, the two went off to the riverbank and fell to, slashing at each other for all they were worth, till both were dead.

I think *boro* may be a recent phenomenon. These days, it is said that their origins were variously called *boronji*, *bonji* or *kanji*.[216] They are like renunciates in appearance, but in fact they are deeply attached to the ego; they appear to yearn for the Buddhist Way, yet they specialize in fighting.

To all appearances these *boro* are shameless and high-handed ruffians, but the complete disregard for death revealed by this story strikes me as impressive, so I decided to set it down as it was told to me.

116

People of old never strove to give special names to temples and all the other things that get named these days, but referred to them quite simply as what they were. Nowadays, it seems, people rack their brains to come up with something that makes them look clever. This is terribly irritating. It is also quite ridiculous to go searching for unusual characters with which to write people's names.

It is the sure mark of a shallow and ignorant person to be drawn to odd curiosities and delight in unusual explanations.

117

There are seven types of people one should not have as a friend.

The first is an exalted and high-ranking person. The second, somebody young. The third, anyone strong and in perfect health. The fourth, a man who loves drink. The fifth, a brave and daring warrior. The sixth, a liar. The seventh, an avaricious man.

The three to choose as friends are – one who gives gifts, a doctor and a wise man.

118

Apparently, the sidelocks remain smooth and unbushy on days when you eat carp broth. It is also used for making glue, so it must be quite glutinous.

The carp is a particularly superior fish, since it is the only fish to be cut and served before His Majesty.

Among fowl, the pheasant is unsurpassed. Pheasant and *matsutake* mushrooms give no offence if hung in the water-heating room,[217] unlike other foods. After seeing a wild goose in the black lacquered cupboard at the empress's palace, the Kitayama Novice[218] went home and sent back a letter saying, 'I have never before seen such a creature lying like that in the black cupboard, exactly as it died, and I found the sight revolting. This must have happened because there is no one worthy in service at your palace.'

119

The fish called 'bonito' is the finest caught in the seas around Kamakura, and is much prized nowadays. An old man in Kamakura told me, 'This fish was never served to the elite until the time we were young. Even the servants wouldn't eat the head, but cut it off and threw it away.'

In these decadent times, such things have penetrated to even the upper echelons.

120

We would be no worse off if we lacked all things Chinese, aside from medicine. Chinese books are widely found in our country now, and are perfectly easy to make copies of. It is quite ridiculous the way such a throng of ships makes the difficult crossing from China, all crammed to the gunwales with useless objects.

After all, the classics speak of 'not prizing things from afar' and 'setting no store by treasure that is hard to come by'.[219]

121

The domestic animals are the horse and the ox. It is a shame to tether the poor things and make them suffer, but it can't be helped, since they are indispensable to us. One should most certainly have a dog, as they are better than men at guarding the house. However, since all the houses around you will have dogs, you probably don't need to go out of your way to get one yourself.

All other creatures, be it bird or beast, are useless. When you lock an animal that runs free into a cage or chain it up, when you snip the wings of a flying bird and confine it, the beast will ceaselessly pine for the wild and the bird for the clouds. Surely no one with a heart to imagine how unbearable he himself would find it could take pleasure in these creatures' torment. It would take the stony heart of a Jie or a Zhou[220] to enjoy witnessing the suffering of a living creature.

Wang Huizhi[221] loved birds. He watched them frolicking happily in the forest, and made them his companions in his rambles. He did not catch them and make them suffer. We should follow the words of the classic:[222] 'Do not cultivate rare birds or strange beasts in your own land.'

122

One's education must first of all be directed to a thorough knowledge of the classics and an understanding of the teachings of the sages. Next, you should learn to write with a fine hand, even if you don't make a specialty of it, as an aid to learning.[223] After this, you should study the medicinal arts. Without these, you cannot look after your own health, help others or perform your filial obligations. Next, you must devote some time to archery and horse riding, skills which are listed among the Six Arts.[224] A knowledge of the classics, the martial arts and medicine is absolutely essential, and no one who studies these can be accused of a useless life.

Next is food, 'man's very heaven', as the saying goes. The knowledge of how to concoct fine flavours must be deemed a fine virtue in a man. And next is fine handiwork, which is useful in all manner of ways.

Aside from these, it is a matter of shame for a gentleman to cultivate too many accomplishments.

Skill in the art of poetry and music is the acknowledged path of the truly refined sensibility, esteemed by ruler and subjects alike, but in our present age they have clearly grown increasingly unrealistic as a means of governing the country – just as gold, for all its glory, cannot compete with all the practical uses of iron.

123

Anyone who wastes time in worthless pursuits must be called a fool or a villain. Obligation compels us to do many things for the sake of lord and nation, and we have little enough time left for ourselves. Think of it like this: we have an inescapable need, first, to acquire food, second, clothes, and third, a place to live. These and these alone are the three great necessities of human life. To live without hunger or cold, sheltered from the elements and at peace – this is happiness.

Yet we are all prey to sickness, and once ill the wretchedness of it is hard to bear, so we should add medical treatment to our list. Thus, we have four things without which a man is poor, while a man who lacks none of these is rich. It is sheer self-indulgence to pursue anything beyond these four. With these four in moderation, no one could be said to lack anything in life.

124

The monk Zehō is among the finest scholars in the Pure Land sect,[225] yet he doesn't parade his learning; he lives in calm seclusion, chanting the *nenbutsu* day in day out. An exemplary existence.

125

A certain holy man who was brought in to perform the forty-ninth-day ceremony after a death[226] gave such a marvellous sermon that everyone present wept. After the holy man had left, those who had heard him exclaimed to each other how especially moving they had found his words today. Then one of them added, 'Yes, and he looks just like a Chinese dog, [227] too,' which quite dispelled the piety and made everyone laugh. Whoever heard of such a way of praising a priest!

Another amusing thing I recall is someone remarking, 'If you drink yourself before pressing sake on your companion, it's like trying to cut someone down with a double-edged sword – in raising it you cut off your own head before you can cut off the other fellow's. He is hardly likely to drink, after all, if you are already staggering drunk yourself.' Had he ever tried this out with a sword, I wonder?

126

Someone once said to me, 'When a man has lost almost everything in gambling,[228] and is preparing to stake all he has left on the next throw, his opponent should withdraw. He should recognize this as the moment when the other's luck is about to change to a winning streak. A good gambler is one who knows when this time has come.'

127

If nothing will be gained by changing something, it is better not to do so.

128

Grand Counsellor Masafusa[229] was a fine, scholarly man, and the retired emperor was planning to promote him to Commander of the Guards, when someone in close service informed His Majesty that he had just witnessed something dreadful.

'What was it?' His Majesty enquired.

'I watched through a gap in the fence as Count Masafusa cut off the leg of a live dog to feed to his hawk,' the man replied.

His Majesty was appalled. The thought of Masafusa revolted him, and he was not promoted after all.

It is extraordinary that such a man would own a hawk, and the story of the dog's leg is absolutely unfounded. The lie was most unfortunate, but how splendid of His Majesty to have reacted with such disgust when he heard the tale.

Overall, it must be said that those who kill or harm living creatures, or set them up to fight each other for their own pleasure, are no better than wild beasts themselves. If you pause and look carefully at the birds and animals, and even the little insects, you will see that they love their children, feel affection for their parents, live in couples, are jealous, angry, full of desire, self-protecting and fearful for their lives, and far more so than men, since they lack all intelligence. Surely one should pity them when they are killed or made to suffer? If you can look on any sentient being without compassion, you are less than human.

129

Yan Hui's firm belief was that he must avoid burdening others.[230] One should not cause suffering and pain to others, nor undermine the will of the humble man.[231]

Some will take pleasure in deceiving, frightening or mocking little children. Adults treat such tales lightly, knowing that they are quite unfounded, but those words will strike deep into the heart of a poor little child, and humiliate, terrify or appal it. It is heartless to enjoy tormenting children in this way.

The joys, angers, sorrows and pleasures of adults too are all based on illusion, but who among us is not attached to the seeming reality of this life?[232]

It harms a man more to wound his heart than to hurt his body. Illness, too, often originates in the mind. Few illnesses come from without. There are times when medicine cannot produce the intended sweat, but shame or fear will always bring one on, which should prove to us that such things come from the mind. We find examples in the classics, after all – think of the man who was hoisted up the Ling Yun Tower to write its signboard, whose hair turned white from fear at the height.[233]

130

It is best to keep the peace with others, bend your own will to conform with theirs and put yourself last and others first.

Those who enjoy the competition of games of every kind do so because they love to win. They delight in their own superior skill. Clearly, then, the loser must feel equivalently downcast. Nor does one derive any enjoyment from choosing to lose in order to please one's competitor. It is unethical to give yourself pleasure by depriving others of it.

When relaxing with close friends, too, some enjoy proving their own wit superior by setting others up and deceiving them. This is most discourteous. Such behaviour has led to much long-standing bitterness, begun innocently enough at a social gathering. All these evils spring from a love of contest.

If you wish to be better than others, you should aim to excel them through study; by pursuing truth, you will learn not to take pride in your virtues or compete with others. It takes the strength conferred by study to enable you to relinquish high office and to turn your back on gain.

131

The poor understand social etiquette in terms of money; the old conceive it in terms of physical strength. Wisdom lies in understanding your own limits, and swiftly relinquishing what lies beyond reach. If someone prevents you, the fault lies with them. If you are ignorant of your limits and persist in the face of them, the fault is your own.

A poor man who fails to accept his poverty will steal; a weak man who does not recognize his weakness will fall ill.

132

The name of the Toba Road does not date from after the Toba Palace was built.[234] It goes back a long way. Apparently there is mention of it in *The Rihō Prince's Diary*,[235] which states that Prince Motoyoshi's recitation of the First Day Felicitations was so magnificent that his voice carried from the Daikokuden[236] all the way to the Toba Road.

133

The emperor's bedding in the imperial bedchamber is placed with the pillow facing east. Sleeping with the head in this direction generally confers dynamic *yang* energy, which is why Confucius also slept thus. Mansions built in the *shinden* style[237] often have the bed facing south.

Retired Emperor Shirakawa slept with head to the north. However, the north should be avoided as inauspicious.[238] Someone also pointed out that the great shrine of Ise[239] lies to the south, and surely it is wrong for His Majesty to lie with feet pointing towards this sacred shrine. When worshipping the distant Ise Shrine, however, the emperor faces not due south but south-east.

134

A certain *samādhi* monk of the Lotus Hall at Retired Emperor Takakura's tomb[240] one day picked up a mirror and took a good look at his face. The shocking ugliness of his own visage filled him with such despair that he found the very mirror repulsive; for a long time afterwards he continued to fear mirrors so much that he wouldn't even touch one, and he avoided the society of others. He secluded himself away, only emerging to take part in the temple's devotions. I was very struck to hear this story.

Even people who seem eminently intelligent will judge others yet have no knowledge of themselves. It makes no sense to lack self-knowledge while understanding those around you. He who knows himself must be said to be the man of real knowledge.

We do not realize that we are ugly, that we are fools, that we are inexpert in our field, worthless, old, a prey to illness, that death is just around the corner, that our Buddhist practice is inadequate. We know nothing of our own faults, let alone of others' criticism of us. Yet we can see ourselves in the mirror. We can count up our years. We do know something of ourselves, yet because we are helpless to change things we could essentially be said to know nothing.

I am not suggesting that we should change our face or make ourselves young again. But why not simply abandon something if you realize your lack of skill? Why not retire to some quiet place and live at ease once you discover you are old? And why, when a man understands that his practice is inadequate, would he not search his soul on the matter?

It is always shameful to mix with those who don't welcome you. A man with an ugly face and poor intelligence will nevertheless go into service, an ignorant man will mingle with the erudite, a talentless fellow will join in with highly skilled practitioners, a white-haired old codger will fraternize with men in their prime; people yearn for the unattainable, bewail matters beyond their power, wait for things that will never come, fear others or fawn on them. The shame in all this is not caused by others. You bring it on yourself by your own greed. This insatiable desire is due to a lack of real understanding that the end of life, that tremendous thing, is at this very moment as good as upon us.

135

Someone called, I think, the Novice Grand Counsellor Sukesue one day encountered the Captain and Consultant Tomouji.[241] 'I could answer any question you like to ask me, whatever it might be,' he remarked.

'You really think so?' said Tomouji.

'Well then, try me,' said Sukesue.

'I don't have any grasp of serious matters,' Tomouji said apologetically, 'so I wouldn't be able to ask about such things. Let me just ask about a silly little everyday matter that puzzles me.'

'Oh, if it's just some trivial little thing I'll have even less trouble clarifying it for you, whatever it may be,' said Sukesue.

The retainers and gentlewomen who were present thought this was a fine idea for a competition, and suggested that the contest might as well be conducted in the imperial presence. It was decided that the loser must provide everyone with a feast.

When they were gathered before His Majesty, Tomouji put the following question: 'I have heard this ever since I was a child but have never understood it. Please explain the meaning of *muma no kitsuriyō kitsu ni no wo ka naka kuboreiri kuren tō*.'[242]

Sukesue was at a complete loss. 'That's just silly,' he declared. 'It's not worth wasting words on.'

'Well, I said all along I knew nothing of deep matters, so we agreed that the question would be about some silly, trivial thing,' Tomouji countered.

So the Grand Counsellor was declared the loser, and the story goes that he paid by providing a splendid feast.

136

Once, when the late Retired Emperor had been served his meal, the imperial physician Atsushige[243] remarked, 'I propose that Your Majesty question me concerning the Chinese characters and efficacy of the various foods just set before you. I will recite the answers from memory, and Your Majesty might check them with reference to the *Herbal Compendium.*[244] I do not think I will make a single mistake.'

The former Palace Minister Rokujō[245] happened to enter just then. 'Let me profit from this knowledge as well,' he said. 'First, what is the left-side radical of the character for "salt"?'[246]

'It is written with the earth radical,' Atsushige replied.

'You have demonstrated your talent sufficiently. I have nothing more to ask,' said the Palace Minister. There was a roar of laughter, and Atsushige left the room.

137

Should we look at the spring blossoms only in full flower, or the moon only when cloudless and clear? To long for the moon with the rain before you, or to lie curtained in your room while the spring passes unseen,[247] is yet more poignant and deeply moving. A branch of blossoms on the verge of opening, a garden strewn with fading petals, have more to please the eye. Could poems on the themes of 'Going to view the blossoms to find them already fallen' or 'Written when I was prevented from going to see the flowers' be deemed inferior to 'On seeing the blossoms'? It is natural human feeling to yearn over the falling blossoms and the setting moon – yet some, it seems, are so insensitive that they will declare that since this branch and that have already shed their flowers, there is nothing worth seeing any longer.

In all things, the beginning and end are the most engaging. Does the love of man and woman suggest only their embraces? No, the sorrow of lovers parted before they met, laments over promises betrayed, long lonely nights spent sleepless until dawn, pining thoughts for one in some far place, a woman left sighing over past love in her tumbledown abode – it is these, surely, that embody the romance of love.

Rather than gazing on a clear full moon that shines over a thousand leagues, it is infinitely more moving to see the moon near dawn and after long anticipation, tinged with most beautiful palest blue, a moon glimpsed among cedar branches deep in the mountains, its light now hidden again by the gathering clouds of an autumn shower. The moist glint of moonlight on the glossy leaves of the forest *shii* oak or the white oak pierces the heart, and makes you yearn for the distant capital and a friend of true sensibility to share the moment with you.

Are blossoms and the moon merely things to be gazed at with the eye? No, it brings more contentment and delight to stay inside the house in spring and, there in your bedroom, let your heart go out to the unseen moonlit night.

The man of quality never appears entranced by anything; he savours things with a casual air. Country bumpkins, however, take flamboyant pleasure in everything. They will wriggle their way in through the crowd and stand there endlessly gaping up at the blossoms, sit about under the trees drinking sake and indulging in linked verse-making together[248] and, finally, oafishly break off great branches of blossom to carry away. They will dip their hands and feet into clear spring water, get down to stand in unsullied snow and leave their footprints everywhere, and in short throw themselves into everything with uninhibited glee.

I have observed such people behaving quite astonishingly when they came to see the Kamo festival. Declaring that the procession was horribly late so there was no point in hanging around on the viewing stand, a group retired to a house behind the stands and settled down to eat, drink and play *go* and *sugoroku*, leaving one of their number back on the stand to keep watch. 'It's coming by!' he shouted, whereupon they all leaped frantically to their feet and dashed back, elbowing each other out of the way as they scrambled up, nearly tumbling off in their eagerness to thrust aside the blinds[249] for a better look, jostling for position and craning to miss nothing, and commenting volubly on everything they saw. Then, when that section of the procession[250] had passed, off they went again, declaring they'd be back for the next one. They were clearly only there to see the spectacle.

The upper echelons from the capital, on the other hand, will sit there dozing without so much as a glance at the scene. Young gentlemen of lesser rank are constantly rising to wait on their superiors, while those seated in the back rows never rudely lean forward, and no one goes out of his way to watch as the procession passes.

On the day of the festival everything is elegantly strewn with the emblematic *aoi* leaves,[251] and even before dawn the carriages quietly begin to arrive to secure a good viewing position, everyone intrigued about which carriage is whose, sometimes identifying them by an accompanying servant or ox-boy they recognize. It is endlessly fascinating to watch the carriages come and go, some charming, others more showy. By the time evening draws in, all those rows of carriages and the people who were crammed into the stands have disappeared, and hardly a soul is left. Once the chaos of departing carriages is over, the blinds and matting are taken down from the stands as you watch, and the place is left bare and forlorn, moving you to a poignant sense of the brevity of worldly things. It is this that is the real point of seeing the festival.[252]

Among the people coming and going in front of the stands there are many you recognize, making you realize there are not really so many people in this world. Even if you were destined to die after all these others, clearly your own death cannot be far away. When a large vessel filled with water is pierced with a tiny hole, though each drop is small it will go on relentlessly leaking until soon the vessel is empty. The city is filled with people, but not a day would go by without someone dying. And is it only one or two a day? There are times when the corpses on the pyres of Toribe, Funaoka[253] and elsewhere further afield are piled high, but no day passes without a funeral. And so the coffin sellers no sooner make one than it is sold. Be they young, be they strong, the time of death comes upon all unawares. It is an extraordinary miracle that we have escaped it until now. Can we ever, even briefly, have peace of mind in this world?

It is like the game of *mamakodate*,[254] played with *sugoroku* pieces, in which no one knows which in the line of pieces will be removed next – when the count is made and a piece is taken, the rest seem to have escaped, but the count goes on and more are picked off in turn, so that no piece is finally spared. Soldiers going into battle, aware of the closeness of death, forget their home and their own safety. And it is sheer folly for a man who lives secluded from the world in his lowly hut, spending his days in idle delight in his garden, to pass off such matters as irrelevant to himself. Do you imagine that the enemy Impermanence will not come forcing its way into your peaceful mountain retreat? The recluse faces death as surely as the soldier setting forth to battle.

138

Someone I knew of had all the *aoi* leaves removed from his reed blinds after the festival, on the grounds that they were of no further use. I thought this was very boorish of him, but since he was a person of quality I wondered whether it was in fact the proper thing to do. However, in her personal poetry collection Suhō no Naishi[255] writes:

How pointless now	*kakuredomo*
these withered leaves that still	*kai naki mono wa*
hang in my blind	*morotomo ni*
since the one I loved is gone	*misu no aoi no*
and cannot see them with me[256]	*kareha narikeri*

which the accompanying preface states was written of the withered festival *aoi* leaves left in the reed blinds surrounding the inner chamber. Another preface from an old poem goes, 'Sent between faded *aoi* leaves'. And in *The Pillow Book* Sei Shōnagon writes: 'Things that make you feel nostalgic – a dried sprig of *aoi*',[257] which is a wonderfully tender image. In his *Tales of the Four Seasons*[258] Kamo no Chōmei writes: 'the remnant *aoi* hangs there yet upon the blind'. Sad enough that it should fade, surely – how could one throw it out without a thought?

The herbal balls hung on the curtained dais in the fifth month stay there until replaced by the ninth-day, ninth-month chrysanthemums,[259] so the iris plants hung with them ought to remain until chrysanthemum time. Ben no Menoto, on seeing the faded iris and herbal balls in the old inner chamber after the Biwa Dowager Empress had died, wrote of 'weeping to leave hanging / these roots out of their time', to which Gō Jijū wrote in response, 'though yet the irises remain'.[260]

139

The trees one wants in a garden are the pine and the cherry. Of the pines, the white pine is good. As for blossoms, the single cherry is best. The double cherry was once found only in the old capital of Nara, but these days it is everywhere, it seems. The cherries of Yoshino and the Left Guard cherry[261] are all single flowers. The double cherry is a peculiar thing, gaudy and distorted, and there is no need to have it in the garden. The late-flowering cherry is also unattractive. It is repulsive to see it crawling with insects.

As for blossoming plums, the white and the pale crimson are best. The single one that flowers early, the double crimson with its lovely smell – all are delightful. The late plum that flowers with the cherry is not so interesting. The cherry blossom overwhelms it, and the sight of the withered blooms on its boughs is also mournful. The Kyōgoku Counsellor Novice[262] planted single-flowering plums close to his eaves, because he was charmed by the impetuous way they flower and scatter before all the other blossom trees. Two of the trees apparently still stand on the south side of his Kyōgoku residence.

Willows are also delightful. The young maple leaves of the fourth month are more beautiful than any flowers or autumn leaves. Both *tachibana* and *katsura*[263] trees should be old and large.

As for plants: the kerria, the wisteria, the iris and the carnation pink. For ponds: the lotus. Plants for autumn: miscanthus reeds, plume grass, the bellflower, the bush clover, yellow valerian, the *fujibakama*, the aster, the burnet, the themeda, the gentian, the white chrysanthemum. Also the yellow chrysanthemum. The ivy, kudzu vine and morning glory should trail over low fences and not be left to grow too high or thick.

It is very hard to feel fond of other plants – rare ones, or those with off-putting Chinesey names or unfamiliar flowers. Generally speaking, the rare and strange are things that please the lower type. It is best not to have them.

140

A sensible man will not die leaving valuables behind. A collection of vulgar objects looks bad, while good ones will suggest a futile attachment to worldly things. And it is even more unfortunate to leave behind a vast accumulation. There will be ugly fights over it after your death, with everyone determined to get things for himself. If you plan to leave something to a particular person, you should pass it on while you are still alive.

Some things are necessary for day-to-day living, but one should have nothing else.

141

The holy man Gyōren of Hiden-in,[264] whose lay name was Miura, was a consummate warrior.

One day, a visitor from his home area remarked that one could trust people from the eastern provinces to speak honestly, but those in the capital were hypocrites, masters of the empty agreement.

But the holy man argued as follows: 'You may think so, but I've lived in the capital for a long time and am quite familiar with people here, and from what I've observed I don't think they are any worse. The folk here are all gentle and soft-hearted, so they find it difficult to come out with a straight refusal to your request. They're not aiming to deceive, it's probably just that there are so many poor folk who are in no position to do as they'd like, so they often can't help you despite wanting to. I'm an Easterner myself, but I do think we are lacking in tenderness and sensitivity. We're blunt and unsophisticated, so we'll give a straight "no" and that's that. It's our wealth and prosperity that make people trust us.'

Gyōren's accent was rough and distorted, and I had always

assumed that he was poorly versed in the finer points of the Buddhist scriptures, but these words drew me to him, and made me realize that his being singled out from among so many monks to be in charge of the temple must have been due to this tender nature of his.

142

Even people who seem to lack any finer feelings will sometimes say something impressive.

An alarming-looking ruffian from the eastern provinces once turned to the man beside him and asked if he had any children. 'Not one,' the man replied.

'Well then,' said the Easterner, 'you'll not know what true depth of feeling is. It frightens me to think of a man unacquainted with tenderness. It's having your own children that brings home to you the poignant beauty of life.'

This is indeed true. Without familial love, would such a man as this be able to feel compassion? Even a man who lacks all filial piety will discover how a parent feels when he himself has children.

It is wrong for a man who has taken the tonsure and cast all away to despise those he sees around him encumbered with worldly ties, who go crawling abjectly after this person and that and are full of craving. If you imagined yourself in his place, you would see how he might abase himself so far as to steal for the sake of his beloved parents or wife and children. Rather than seizing thieves and punishing their crimes, it would be better to make the world a place where people did not go hungry or cold. A man without stable means is a man whose heart is unstable. People steal from extremity. There will be no end to crime while the world is not governed well, and men suffer from cold and starvation. It is cruel to make people suffer and drive them to break the law, then treat the poor creatures as criminals.

As for how to improve people's lives, there can be no doubt that it would benefit those below if people in high positions were to cease their luxurious and wasteful ways and instead were kind and tender to the people, and encouraged agriculture. The true criminal must be defined as a man who commits a crime though he is as decently fed and clothed as others.

143

When someone reports that a man has died a fine death, one would be impressed enough with the modest statement that he died peacefully and without distress – but fools will go on to add details about the man's strange or unusual appearance at the time, or elaborately praise his deathbed words or gestures to suit their own fancy, making you doubt that this is the same man as he would have been in life.

Even an avatar of the Buddha himself is in no position to pronounce on this great event, nor can the wisest scholar gauge it. Enough that the man himself dies without error – a death should not be judged by what others may have witnessed.

144

Once, when the holy man of Toganowo[265] was travelling along a road, he overheard a man who was washing his horse in a stream instructing the horse to lift its leg with the words '*Ashi! Ashi!*'[266]

The saint came to a standstill. 'How marvellous!' he exclaimed. 'This fellow's virtue in a previous lifetime has brought him to enlightenment! Hear how he cries "*Aji! Aji!*" Whose horse is this, pray? Ah, wonderful beyond words!'

'It belongs to the Fushō,'[267] replied the man.

'Marvellous! He speaks of *aji hon fushō*! What virtue I have gained from this encounter!'[268] exclaimed the holy man, wiping tears of joy from his eyes.

145

The imperial bodyguard Hada no Shigemi[269] once said of one of the retired emperor's guard, the Shimotsuke Novice Shingan,[270] 'He has the mark of one prone to falling from horses.

He should take great care.' Shingan thought this very unlikely, but he did indeed fall from his horse and die. Everyone then decided that the words issuing from such an expert in his field were divinely prophetic.

So just what was this mark? people asked him. 'He showed all the signs by having a very poor riding seat, and favouring horses that tend to buck,' replied the guard. 'Have I ever been wrong?'

146

Abbot Meiun[271] asked a man skilled in readings of physiognomy whether he was in danger of harm from a weapon.

'You do indeed have such a sign,' replied the physiognomist.

'What sign is that?' asked the monk.

'Your position makes it unlikely that you would come to such harm,' the man replied, 'but the fact that it has occurred to you to ask such a question portends danger.' And sure enough, he was killed by an arrow.

147

Recently, people have begun to say that too many moxibustion scars make a person unfit to perform worship before the gods.[272] There is no mention of this in the old laws and regulations.

148

If someone over forty has moxibustion they may grow faint unless moxa is placed on the Three *Ri*.[273] It is essential that this be done.

149

One shouldn't put new deer antler[274] to the nose and sniff it. There is a tiny insect in it that will enter through the nose and devour the brain.

150

People who are learning an art generally claim that it is best not to inadvertently let others know about your attempts until you are accomplished. The way to really impress is to polish your craft in secret before making it public. But someone who says such things will never acquire any art.

A person who mingles with skilled practitioners while he himself is still inexpert, and isn't ashamed of their ridicule and laughter but calmly and devotedly perseveres in his practice even if he has no special gift, will continue to progress and not grow lax with the passing years, and will finally outdo the man of talent who lacks dedication. He will attain mastery in his art, continue to increase his skill and gain an unequalled reputation in his field.

Some truly great practitioners were reviled for their lack of skill when they first began, and indeed had dreadful faults. But in every art we find the same thing – such a man has maintained a deep respect for the rules of his art, and not indulged his own whims, with the result that he has become a renowned master who draws crowds of disciples to his door.

151

Somebody has remarked that if you have not become adept at an art by the time you are fifty, you should give up. You do not have the time left to make further efforts worthwhile.

People should not laugh at the old. It is painful and off-putting to see old men mixing with society. As a rule, those over fifty are most seemly when they withdraw from all activities and retire to a leisured life, and this is what they ought to do. A man is a fool if he spends his entire life involved with worldly affairs. If there is something you wish to know, by all means ask instruction of others, but once you have grasped the facts well enough to feel clear about the question, pursue it no further. The ideal is not to desire to know in the first place.

152

The holy priest Jōnen of Saidaiji Temple[275] once called at the Inner Palace.

'What a wonderfully saintly figure!' the Saionji Palace Minister[276] exclaimed on seeing Jōnen's venerable appearance – the bent back, the snowy brows.

The Palace Minister's air of veneration prompted Count Suketomo[277] to remark, 'It's simply that he's old.'

The story has it that some days later Count Suketomo arrived with a hideously decrepit and balding shaggy dog in tow, which he presented to the Palace Minister with the words, 'A fine saintly figure, don't you think?'

153

When Grand Counsellor Novice Tamekane was surrounded by a throng of soldiers, arrested and taken to the Rokuhara Commissary,[278] Count Suketomo observed the incident from the vicinity of Ichijō Street.

'Ah, how I envy him,' he remarked. 'That's the ideal kind of memory to take from having lived.'[279]

154

One day, Count Suketomo took shelter from the rain under the eaves of the gate of Tōji Temple,[280] where cripples had gathered. Observing how strange and deformed they were with their warped and twisted limbs, some turned right back on themselves, it struck him that they were all quite unique and extraordinary, and should be more deeply appreciated. But as he continued to gaze at them his interest quickly waned, and he began to find them ugly and disgusting. There is actually nothing better than straightforward, unexceptional things, he decided.

He had recently developed a pleasure in potted plants, and particularly enjoyed acquiring those that were twisted in unusual ways, but when he went home and saw them now it struck him that this was no different from his interest in the cripples. They lost all charm for him, and he had every one dug up and thrown away.

Precisely so.

155

If you would take the world on its own terms, you need above all to read the mood of the moment. If the timing isn't right, your words will grate on your listeners and upset them, and your plans will come to nothing. You must know how to recognize such occasions.

There is no choosing your moment, however, when it comes to illness, childbirth or death. You cannot call these things off because 'the time isn't right'. The truly momentous events of life – the changes from birth through life, transformation and death – are like the powerful current of a raging river. They surge ever forward without a moment's pause. Thus, when it comes to the essentials, both in religious and in worldly life, you should not wait for the right moment in what you wish to achieve, nor dawdle over preparations. Your feet must never pause.

Summer does not come once spring is done, nor autumn arrive at the end of summer. Spring begins early to hold summer's intimations, while hints of autumn already come and go within summer, and no sooner is autumn here than winter's cold begins. The tenth month, winter's start, has a spring-like warmth that greens the plants and swells the buds on the plum. The leaves of trees, too, do not fall before the new shoots begin. They fall unable to withstand the pressure from beneath, where the young leaves are already forming. The tree is prepared and waiting from within, and so each change presses swiftly forward.

Still swifter are the changes through human life, from birth to old age, sickness and death. The seasons progress in a fixed order. Not so the time of death. We do not always see its approach; it can come upon us from behind. People know that they will die, but death will surprise them while they believe it is not yet close. It is as if we gaze at the far-off ebb-tide flats while even now the sea is rising to flood the rocks we stand on.

156

It is the custom for a newly appointed minister to borrow some suitably fine place in which to hold his inauguration banquet. The Uji Minister of the Left[281] held his at the Higashi Sanjō Palace. The emperor was in residence there when the request was made, so His Majesty removed to a different place for the occasion.

Apparently it is an ancient custom to borrow the empress dowager's residence, though there is no particular reason for this.

157

To take up the brush is to write, to take up an instrument is to feel the urge to make it sing. A sake cup in the hand provokes the thought of sake, while a dice in your palm will prompt ideas of gambling. Contact will always trigger the associated urge. Never for a moment indulge in wrongful pastimes.

A passing glance at a phrase from the holy teachings will lead the eye on to read the words surrounding it, and before you know it you may have righted years of error. Had you not opened the text just then, you might never have had that realization. This is an example of the virtue of contact. Even if you lack all faith, simply to seat yourself before an image, hold a rosary and take up a sutra book is to perform a virtuous act, however perfunctory; even seated on your meditation chair with distracted mind, you will sink into meditation before you know it.

Phenomena and their essence are intrinsically one. If outward actions conform, inner realization will naturally follow. Do not decry a lack of faith – such 'empty gestures' in fact deserve our reverence.

158

A certain nobleman was kind enough to ask my interpretation of the practice of tossing away any undrunk sake before offering the cup to another.

'I believe the term for it, *gyōtō*, means "collecting at the bottom", the implication being that it should be thrown away,' I replied.

'No,' he said, 'the expression is actually written with characters meaning "fish road". Its meaning is to leave a little sake in the cup with which to rinse the rim where your lips have been.'[282]

159

Someone exalted once informed me that the word *minamusubi*,[283] a style of cording, derives from the similarity to the shell known as a *mina*. It is a mistake to pronounce it '*nina*'.

160

Is it wrong to speak of hanging a sign on the gate[284] as 'nailing' it there? The Kadenokōji Second-rank Novice[285] used to say 'hang'. And is it similarly wrong to speak of 'nailing up' viewing stands? It is common to use the expression in the case of nailing up temporary awnings,[286] but for viewing stands 'instal' is the correct term. It is also wrong to speak of 'burning' a sacred *goma* fire.[287] The verb should be 'to perform the ritual' or 'to *goma*'.

The bishop of Seikanji has told me that it is wrong to pronounce the word *gyōbō*, with the soft 'h', as *gyōhō*.[288]

There are many such examples in words we commonly use.

161

People say that the cherry blossoms are at their full one hundred and fifty days after the winter solstice, or sometimes that this occurs seven days after the spring equinox, but it is generally correct to say it is seventy-five days after the first day of spring.[289]

162

One of the general duties monks at Henzōji Temple[290] was in the habit of taming the water birds that came to the temple pond, spreading food for them right into the hall and leaving the door open. When a great flock had gathered inside he went in after them, shut them in and proceeded to catch and kill them.

Some children who were cutting grass nearby heard the terrible hubbub. They told the villagers, and the men rose up in a body and forced their way into the hall. They found the monk in the midst of a crowd of big wild geese that were desperately flapping about, grabbing birds, pinning them down and wringing their necks. They seized him and took him to police headquarters. He was thrown into jail, with the birds he had killed hung round his neck.

This happened in the time when Grand Counsellor Mototoshi[291] was Director of Police.

163

Those versed in Yin-Yang divination once argued over the question of which way to write the 'tai' in the alternative name for the ninth month, Taishō, some saying it should have the extra stroke[292] and others disagreeing. Novice Morichika advised that the Konoe Chancellor[293] had in his possession an imperial diary written on the back of a divination report in the hand of Yoshihira himself,[294] in which the extra stroke was used.

164

When people get together they are never silent for a moment. They will always talk. When you listen to what they say, a great deal of it is pointless. There is much harm and little good for either party in such worldly gossip and judgement of others. But as they talk, they are unaware how futile for both of them this chatter is.

165

It is unseemly to mix with those who are not from one's own world – for a man from the eastern provinces to mix with people from the capital, or someone from the capital to establish himself in the East, or for a monk from either the esoteric or exoteric schools[295] to leave his own sect.

166

The way people struggle to get along in the world strikes me as like fashioning a buddha from snow on a spring day, decking it out with precious metals and jewels, then setting out to build a worship hall for it. Would it survive long enough to be placed in the finished hall?

So many strive in hopes of the future, even as the life still in them is daily dissolving away like snow from beneath the snowman.

167

Often a practitioner of one art will attend a performance of another one and, either aloud or in his heart, bemoan the fact that if only it were his own field he would not be sitting on the sidelines in this fashion. But this seems to me very wrong. If he hankers after another of the arts, he should simply say, 'Oh dear, why didn't I take that up myself?'

To parade your own knowledge and pit it against others is like a horned beast lowering its head at an opponent, or a fanged animal baring its teeth.

It is a virtue in a man to be humble about his own merits and not vie with others. A sense of superiority to others is very wrong. One who considers himself superior through birth, skill or eminent forebears, even if he never expresses this, is full of error in his heart. One should take care to put such things out of one's mind. There is nothing like pride for making a man look a fool, provoking criticism from others and inviting disaster. One truly skilled in his art will be all too aware of his own faults and thus never satisfied with himself, which means he will never be proud.

168

Sometimes an old man has developed an exceptional skill in some field, and no one can imagine who they will all turn to once he has died. This is a man who justifies old age, and whose continued existence is worthwhile. Nevertheless, you could also deplore his continued vigour, on the grounds that it is owing to a long and single-minded devotion to one thing. Better for the old to say indifferently, 'I no longer remember any of that.'

Generally speaking, even though you may know a great deal, if you go around parading it people will doubt that you are as good as you make out. Besides, one inevitably makes mistakes. The man who claims not to really understand is more likely to be thought a true master of his art.

More painful still is to sit there thinking, 'That's quite wrong!' as you listen to the self-satisfied pontifications of someone who doesn't know what he is talking about but is too exalted to be criticized.

169

Somebody remarked that the term *shiki* was always used alone until the time of Gosaga's reign, but these days it is often combined with something else.[296] When Ukyō no Daibu, gentlewoman to Kenreimon'in, returned to serve at the palace after Gotoba acceded to the throne, she wrote 'for all that the *shiki* there remained unchanged . . .'[297]

170

It is not good to call on someone if you have no particular reason. Even if you go with some purpose, you should leave promptly once your business is accomplished. It is very annoying if a visit drags on.

There is so much talking when people get together. It is exhausting, disturbs the peace of mind and wastes time better spent on other things. There is nothing to be gained for either party. It is bad, too, to feel irritable as you talk. When you don't care for something, you should come right out and say so.

The exception to all this is when someone after your own heart, whom you feel inclined to talk with, is at a loose end and encourages you to stay a while longer for a peaceful chat. No doubt we all have Ruan Ji's 'welcoming green eyes'[298] from time to time.

It is very nice when a friend simply drops in, has a quiet talk with you, and then leaves. It is also wonderfully pleasing to receive a letter that simply begins, 'I write because it's been some time since I sent news,' or some such.

171

If someone engaged in a game of shell matching[299] neglects the shells in front of him while he looks around to check what others might be hiding in their sleeves or by their knees, his own shells will be snatched from in front of him. Those who are good at the game seem not to go to the length of taking shells from distant players but limit themselves to those close at hand, yet they manage to acquire a large number.

When you place a piece at the corner of the *go* board, you will fail to hit the piece you are aiming for if you look at it as you flick it.[300] You should carefully watch where your hand is, and send the piece straight through the closest black circle.[301] Then you will be sure to hit the other piece.

In all things, do not seek for distant advantage. Simply maintain correctly what is close to hand. In the words of the Chinese sage Duke Xiao of Qing,[302] 'Do what is good, and ask no questions of the future.' Surely a ruler should also govern in this way. If he fails to attend to internal affairs and acts with careless irresponsibility, the more distant parts of his realm will inevitably rebel, and only then will he reach for controlling measures – as the *Book of Medicine*[303] says, only a fool would pray to the gods for a cure while exposing himself to wind and sleeping in the damp. Such people do not realize that by alleviating the suffering of those before your eyes, practising benevolence and living rightly, your good influence will extend far beyond. The legendary emperor Yu did far better in withdrawing his armies and governing virtuously, than in setting off to defeat the Miao.[304]

172

A young man overflows with vigour, things stir his heart, and he is prone to passions. Like a flung ball, such a youth courts danger and physical harm. Riches are wasted in pursuit of magnificence, then all this is suddenly abandoned for the wretched robes of the monk; he is full of fervour and fight, suffers agonies of shame or bitterness, and his fancies are constantly shifting from day to day. He will devote himself to women and pursue infatuations, or take his example from those who have died with no thought to their own safety or longevity, behaving with such reckless daring that 'a long life lies ruined',[305] or let himself be drawn wherever his heart urges, becoming the cause of talk for many years to come. It is indeed in youth that we make our mistakes.

In age, on the other hand, the spirit weakens, we become indifferent and apathetic, and nothing rouses us. The heart grows naturally calm, so that we no longer act in futile ways but instead tend to our bodies, live free of discontent and try to avoid troubling others. Age has more wisdom than youth, just as youth has more beauty than does age.

173

Almost nothing is known for certain about the poet Ono no Komachi. She is described in decrepit old age in the document known as *Tamatsukuri*. Some say it was written by Kiyoyuki, but it is recorded as being among the writings of the saint of Mount Kōya, Kōbō Daishi.[306] He passed away at the beginning of the Jōwa era, but it seems that Ono no Komachi flourished after that time. It is all very confusing.

174

It is said that a dog used for hunting with small hawks will be spoiled for this sport if used with large hawks.[307] This holds a universal truth – follow the great, and you will abandon the small.

Among all the many things in life, nothing is more fulfilling than delighting in the Way. This is indeed the truly great thing. What can you not relinquish when once you have heard of and committed yourself to the Way of Buddhism? To what else could you devote your energies? Even a fool is surely wiser than a clever dog.

175

There are many incomprehensible things in this world.

I cannot understand why people will seize any occasion to immediately bring out the sake, delighting in forcing someone else to drink. The other will frown and grimace in painful protest, attempt to throw it away when no one's looking or do his best to escape, but this man will seize him, pin him down and make him swallow cup after cup. A genteel man will quickly be transformed into a madman and start acting the fool; a vigorous, healthy fellow will before your very eyes become shockingly afflicted and fall senseless to the floor. What a thing to do, on a day of celebration! Right into the next day his head hurts, he can't eat, and he lies there groaning with all memory of the previous day gone as if it were a former life. He neglects essential duties both public and private, with disastrous effects. It is both boorish and cruel to subject someone to this sort of misery. Surely a man who has had this bitter experience will be filled with regret and loathing. Anyone from a land that lacked this custom would be amazed and appalled to hear of its existence in another country.

It is depressing enough just to witness this happening to another. A man who had always seemed thoughtful and refined will burst into mindless laughter, prattle on and on, his lacquered court cap askew, the ties of his robes loosened and the skirts hauled up above his shins, and generally behave so obliviously that he seems a changed man. A woman will blatantly push her hair up away from her face, throw back her head and laugh quite shamelessly, and seize the hand of the person with the sake, while the more uncouth might grab one of the snacks and hold it to someone else's mouth or eat it herself – a quite disgraceful sight. People bellow at the top of their lungs, everyone sings and prances about, and an old monk is called in, who proceeds to bare his filthy black shoulder and writhe about so that you can hardly stand to watch, and you loathe just as much the others who sit there enjoying the spectacle.

Some will make you cringe by the way they sing their own praises, others will cry into their drink, while the lower orders abuse each other and get into quite shocking and appalling fights. Finally, after all manner of disgraceful and pitiful behaviour, the drunkard will seize things without permission, then end up hurting himself by rolling off the veranda or tumbling from his horse or carriage. If he's of a class that goes on foot he'll stagger away down the high road, doing unspeakable things against people's walls or gates as he goes. It is quite disgusting to see the old monk in his black robe stumbling off, steadying himself with his hand on the shoulder of the lad beside him and rambling on incomprehensibly.

If drinking like this profited us in this world or the next, what could one say? But in this world it leads to all manner of error, and causes both illness and loss of wealth. Wine has been called 'the greatest of medicines',[308] but in fact all sickness springs from it. It is claimed that you forget your sorrows in drink, but from what I can see, men in their cups will in fact weep to recall their past unhappiness. As for the next world – having lost the wisdom you were born with, reduced all your good karma to ashes, built up a store of wickedness and broken all the Buddhist precepts, you are destined for hell. Remember, the Buddha teaches that those who lift the wine glass either to their own lips or to others' will spend five hundred lifetimes without hands.[309]

Yet, loathsome though one finds it, there are situations when a cup of sake is hard to resist. On a moonlit night, a snowy morning, or beneath the flowering cherry trees, it increases all the pleasures of the moment to bring out the sake cups and settle down to talk serenely together over a drink. It is also a great comfort to have a drink together if an unexpected friend calls round when time is hanging heavy on your hands. And it is quite wonderful when sake and snacks are elegantly served from behind her curtains by some remote and exalted lady.

It is also quite delightful to sit across from a close friend in some cosy little nook in winter, roasting food over the coals and drinking lots of sake together. And delightful too on a journey to sit about on the grass together in some wayside hut or out in the wild, drinking and lamenting the lack of a suitable snack. And it's a fine thing when someone who really hates having sake pressed on them is forced to have just a little. You are thrilled when some grand person singles you out and offers to refill your cup, urging, 'Do have more. You've barely drunk.' And it is also very pleasing when someone you would like to get to know better is a drinker and becomes very pally with you in his cups.

All things considered, a drunkard is so entertaining he can be forgiven his sins. Think of the charming scene when a master throws open the door on his servant, who is sound asleep next morning after an exhausting night on the drink. The poor befuddled fellow rushes off, rubbing his bleary eyes, topknot exposed on his hatless head, only half dressed and clutching the rest of his trailing clothes, his hairy shins sticking out below his lifted skirts as he scampers into the distance – a typical drunk.

176

The room in the palace known as the Black Door[310] has an interesting story attached. When the Komatsu emperor ascended the throne,[311] he did not forget his former days of lowly status when he had indulged in making his own meals there,[312] and he continued the habit. Soot from the firewood burned there blackened the wood of the door, hence the name.

177

Once, when a game of kickball was to be played at the palace of the Kamakura Central Affairs Bureau Prince,[313] there was discussion over what to do about the ground, which was still wet from recent rain. The Oki Governor Novice Sasaki[314] presented a large cartload of sawdust, which was spread over the garden and solved the problem of the mud. 'What impressive foresight to have it at the ready like that,' everyone said admiringly.

When someone told this story, the Yoshisada Middle Captain[315] remarked, 'Was there no dry sand laid by for such an occasion?' How shaming. We had all been impressed by the sawdust, but in fact it was quite vulgar and inappropriate. It seems that the old custom was always for the person in charge of the grounds to keep a store of sand.

178

Some retainers of a certain high-class establishment, describing how they had seen *kagura* dancing in the Sacred Mirror Room at the palace, mentioned that the dancer was holding the Sacred Sword.[316] A gentlewoman overheard this from within her curtains and murmured, 'Yet the sword used on occasions when His Majesty proceeds to another part of the palace is that of the Imperial Day Chamber.'[317] Admirably spoken. The lady had apparently long been in attendance on the emperor.

179

The holy priest Dōgen, a monk who crossed to China in search of teachings, brought back a copy of the Complete Sutras, which he set up for worship at a place called Yakeno near Rokuhara, naming the temple that housed them Naranda, and singling out the *Surangama Samadhi Sutra*[318] to lecture on.

He once remarked, 'Tradition states that the Ōe Governor[319] claimed the main gate of Nālandā Temple in India faced north, but no supporting evidence had been found in any documents, including the *Xi yi* and *Fa Xian*.[320] It was unclear on what authority the governor had made his pronouncement. 'Needless to say,' he added, 'Xi Ming Monastery[321] in China faces north.'

180

The ceremony known as Sagichō involves carrying from the Shingon-in to the Shinsen Garden in the palace[322] the mallets used in the New Year games, and ritually burning them there. The cry 'The Law-fulfilling Pond!'[323] refers to the pond of the Shinsen Garden.

181

A knowledgeable person tells me that the word 'snowdust' in the children's song 'Fly snowdust fly, snowdust of Tamba' derives from the resemblance of fine snow to the dust that flies about during rice hulling. 'Tamba' is apparently a mistake for *tamare*,[324] a word bidding the snow to lie, and the song should continue with the words 'on hedge and branching bough'. It must be an old song. The tale of how Retired Emperor Toba sang it as a child when it was snowing is recorded in *The Diary of Sanuki no Suke*.[325]

182

The Shijo Grand Counsellor Count Takachika[326] once presented dried salmon for the emperor's meal. Overhearing someone remark that such vulgar stuff should not be served to His Majesty,[327] the Grand Counsellor responded, 'I could understand this if salmon itself were never served, but since this is not the case, what can be so wrong about the unsalted and dried form? Is sweetfish not served dried and unsalted to His Majesty, after all?'

183

You can tell if an ox has horned someone because its horns have been cut, while a horse that bites will have its ears lopped off. It is the fault of the owner if an unmarked animal harms someone. One should not keep a dog that bites people. All these things are offences, and forbidden by ancient law.

184

The Matsushita nun[328] was the mother of Tokiyori, Governor of Sagami.[329]

When the Governor was to visit, she set about tidying up the soot-covered paper screen doors, taking up the knife herself to cut away the torn squares and repapering them. Her brother, Castle Deputy Yoshikage,[330] who was there to assist, suggested she put him in charge of the work. 'I'll have one of my men do it,' he said. 'He knows how to do this sort of thing.'

'I'm sure his work would be no better than mine,' she replied, and she went on repairing each ripped square in turn.[331]

Yoshikage then suggested it would be much easier to replace all the paper at once. 'Surely it's unsightly to have some squares new and some old and dirty?' he said.

'I plan to do a thorough replacement job later,' she replied, 'but I'm intentionally leaving them looking like this for today, in order to make a young man understand that, in using things, one only fixes the parts that are damaged.' What a wonderful thing to say!

Thrift is the basis of good government. Though a woman, the nun partook of the wisdom of the sages. She was indeed no ordinary woman, but one who had a ruler of the land for her own son.

185

Castle Deputy and Governor of Mutsu Yasumori[332] was a consummate horseman.

Watching a horse led out for him from the stable, he noted that it crossed the threshold sill by placing its forelegs together and jumping lightly over. 'This horse is too spirited,' he said, and had another saddled instead.

On another occasion, he saw that a horse knocked the sill with its hoof as it stepped forward to cross. 'This horse is too slow-witted,' he said. 'It will cause an accident,' and he chose not to ride it.

Would someone not thoroughly versed in the art be as cautious as this?

186

A horseman by the name of Yoshida once told me, 'All horses are formidable creatures. One should know better than to pit one's strength against a horse's. Before you mount, take a good look at the horse you'll be riding, and learn his strengths and weaknesses. Next, check that the bit and saddle are safe. If anything worries you, don't gallop him. A real rider will never forget these precautions. This is one of the secrets of the art.'

187

A professional in any field will always be superior to a skilful amateur, even if he is not truly accomplished. This is because freedom and impulse cannot equal meticulous care and prudence.

This is so not just of the arts and professions, but of all actions and questions of judgement – a careful fool is on the road to success; one who is skilful but headstrong is headed for failure.

188

A man decided to make his son a monk. 'Study the laws of karmic cause and effect,' he told him, 'and make your living by preaching.'

The lad did as instructed.. First, in order to be a successful preacher, he learned how to ride a horse – he had no palanquin or carriage, after all, and it seemed to him that, if his services were called for and a horse were sent to fetch him, it would be a sorry business if he had a bad riding seat and fell off. Next, he learned some popular songs, for a monk can be regaled with sake after the service is over, and the client would be very unimpressed if he couldn't entertain the gathering[333] in some way. When he had finally gained some competence in these two skills he felt the urge to improve them further, and in the end he grew old having devoted all his time to them with none to spare for learning how to actually preach.

He is not the only one; all of us have this experience. While we are young, we have all manner of ambitious plans for the future – to make a success of ourselves in life, achieve grand things, learn skills, study. But there seems plenty of time to fulfil our wishes, and we dawdle on the way, letting ourselves be distracted by the passing concerns of everyday life, so that we grow old having in fact done nothing much. Regret them as we might, there is no regaining our lost years, and, like a wheel running ever faster downhill, debility overtakes us, while we have succeeded in learning no skill and never achieved the success we dreamed of in life.

Thus, you should carefully consider which among the main things you want in life is the most important, and renounce all the others to dedicate yourself to that thing alone. Among the many matters that press in on us on any day, at any given moment, we must give ourselves to the most productive, by no matter how little – ignore the rest, and devote yourself entirely to the most important thing. If you find yourself reluctant to abandon the others, you will never achieve your primary aim.

It is like a *go* player who never wastes a move, but gets the better of his opponent by sacrificing the small in favour of the large. Here, it is easy to sacrifice three stones to gain ten, but not so easy if you must lose ten to gain eleven. He should always pursue a course that gains him more, even if it is a single extra stone, but when the profit is so marginal a player is often loath to sacrifice the ten precious stones he has accumulated. The urge to cling to one thing while grasping for another will cause the loss of both.

If a man in the capital has urgent business in the eastern hills, but once he arrives at the door realizes that he would gain more by going to the western hills, he should turn around then and there and go west. 'Now that I'm here, I may as well finish my business in the East,' he may think. 'After all, no day was fixed for that other matter. I'll make a decision about it once I'm home.' But the moment's lazy impulse will lead to a lifetime's negligence. You must be very wary of this.

Once you are committed to achieving your one aim, there is no use grieving over the failure of the others. Nor should you be ashamed to be mocked by others. Unless you forego the many, you will not attain that one great thing.

Here is a strange and marvellous tale: someone at a gathering mentioned that there were varying names for types of plume grass, such as *masaho* and *masoho*, and added that the holy man of Watanabe knew the poetic teachings on this matter. The monk Tōren[334] was among those who heard this.

It was raining at the time. 'Can someone lend me a raincoat and rain hat?' he said. 'I'm off to find this holy man and learn the details of this matter from him.'

'No need to be so hasty,' people said. 'Wait till the rain's over.'

'Don't be ridiculous,' replied Tōren. 'Does a man's life wait for a break in the weather? I may die, the holy man may die, and then there would be no chance to ask.' Whereupon he hurried off, and the story goes that he received his answer.

'Swiftness will always bear fruit,'[335] as the work known as the *Analects* says. We should seize the moment to turn our thoughts to that one great matter of the Buddhist Truth with the same alacrity with which Tōren pursued his urge to learn about the plume grass.

189

You can decide to do something today, but before you manage it some unexpected and urgent business will arise to overwhelm your plan for the day, or the person you are waiting for is unable to come, or someone unexpected arrives, or something you were relying on turns out differently, so that the only things that go well are things you hadn't anticipated. Matters that threatened to be difficult prove easy, while those that should be straightforward turn out to cause you great pains. The progress of each passing day is quite unlike your anticipation of it. And the same goes for a year – and for a life.

Yet if you assume that everything you anticipate will go awry, you find that in fact some things don't, which makes it all the more difficult to plan. The only certain truth to learn is that all is uncertain.

190

The one thing a man should not have is a wife.

One is impressed to hear that a certain man always lives alone, while someone who is reported to have married into this or that family, or to have taken a wife and be living together, will find himself quite looked down on. 'He must have married that nondescript girl because he thought she was something special,' people will say scornfully, or if she is a good woman they will think, 'He'll be so besotted that he treats her like his own personal buddha.'[336] The impression is even more dreary when she runs the house well. It is depressing to watch her bear children and fuss over them, and things don't end with his death, for then you have the shameful sight of her growing old and decrepit as a nun.

No matter who the woman may be, you would grow to hate her if you lived with her and saw her day in day out, and the woman must become dissatisfied too. But if you lived separately and sometimes visited her, your feelings for each other would surely remain unchanged through the years. It keeps the relationship fresh to just drop in from time to time on impulse and spend the night.

191

What a shame it is to hear someone declare that things lose their beauty at night! All lustre, ornamentation and brilliance come into their own at night.

In daylight, one can keep things simple and dress sedately. But the best clothing for night is showy and dazzling formal wear. The same goes for people – a good-looking person will look still finer by lamplight, and it's charming to hear a careful voice speaking in darkness. Scents and music too are still lovelier at night.

It is a fine thing to see a man who calls on some great household looking his best late on an uneventful evening. Young people who pay attention to such things will always notice one's appearance no matter what the hour, so it is wise to dress well whatever the situation, whether formal or informal, and most especially at times when one is inclined to relax and unwind. Particularly delightful is when a fine gentleman has bothered to plaster down his hair though it is after dark, or when a lady slips from the room late at night to take up a mirror and see to her face before rejoining the company.

192

It is also good to visit a shrine or temple at night, on days when other pilgrims do not go.

193

An ignorant person will always be wrong when he sizes up another and believes he can judge the other's intelligence.

It is a grave mistake for a foolish fellow who has to his credit the single fact that he is very good at the art of *go*, to decide that an intelligent man who happens to have no skill at *go* is therefore his intellectual inferior, or for someone skilled in any of the crafts to think himself superior because others do not understand his specialty. Scholar priests who know nothing of meditation, and meditation monks who eschew scholarship, are both wrong to judge each other as inferior.

One should never feel rivalry towards those in other fields, or pass judgement on them.

194

A person of powerful understanding will never misread others.

For example, when someone deceives the world around him with lies, there are those who will innocently take him at his word. Others may be so taken in that they make matters worse by embroidering further with their own imaginings. Others again will listen quite unconcernedly and take no interest. Someone else will feel a bit suspicious, and ponder the matter, half inclined to disbelieve. Another might not think it sounds like the truth, but do nothing about it on the grounds that if someone claims such things they might just be true. Another will try to make sense of it in one way or another, nod and smile as if he understands perfectly, and have no clue at all in fact. Yet another will ponder the matter and decide that yes, it must be so, but still worry that it could be mistaken. Another will clap his hands and laughingly declare that there's really nothing peculiar in it at all. Another will be aware that it's a lie but not say so, making no comment on the points he realizes are clearly false but going along with it all just like the rest. And another will have understood just what the liar was up to from the beginning but makes no attempt to show him up, and instead takes his part and helps the lie along.

Even in this sort of instance of idle mischief-making among fools, anyone in the know will clearly understand from words and faces how each of these others is reacting, while a man of real wisdom can observe us bewildered fools as clearly as if we sat in the palm of his hand.

However, such judgements cannot be applied in the same way to Buddhist teachings.[337]

195

Once someone passing along the Koga–Nawate road[338] saw a man dressed in the narrow-sleeved under-coat and wide-skirted under-trousers of a nobleman, who was diligently washing a wooden statue of Jizō[339] in the water of a rice paddy. As the man watched, puzzled, two or three men in courtier's hunting costume arrived. 'Here he is!' they cried, and led him away. It was Palace Minister Koga.[340]

When he was in his right mind, he was a splendid and admirable man.

196

This same gentleman was Commander[341] at the time when the sacred palanquin was returned to Tōdaiji from the Wakamiya Shrine in Tōji.[342] The Minamoto nobles[343] were assembled for the occasion, and Michimoto cleared the way ahead of the procession.

'Is it really necessary to clear the way around the shrine area?' enquired the Tsuchimikado Minister of State.[344]

Michimoto merely replied, 'It is the business of a military family to understand how imperial bodyguards should behave.'

He later remarked that, although the Minister of State had read the *Hokuzanshō*, he had no knowledge of the explanation in the *Saikyūki*.[345] In fact, he went on, one should take particular care to clear the way at shrines for fear of the evil demons and deities that attach themselves to the god's retinue.

197

The term *jōgaku* not only refers to monks in the various temples, but in the *Engishiki*[346] is used of female palace servants. This term doubtless refers in general to lower officials whose numbers were fixed by tradition.

198

There is not only a court post with the name of Nominal Deputy Provincial Governor, but something known as Nominal Fourth-rank Provincial Governor. The record of this is found in the *Seiji Yōryaku*.[347]

199

Abbot Gyōsen of Yokawa[348] once told me that Chinese music is in the mode known as *ryo*, and has no *ritsu* mode,[349] whereas Japan has only the *ritsu* mode.

200

The black or Chinese bamboo has narrow leaves, while the river bamboo has broad ones. River bamboo is the one that grows near the stream in the Imperial Palace; Chinese bamboo is planted along the side of the Jijūden.[350]

201

Of the two stupas known as Taibon and Gejō,[351] the Gejō was the outer and the Taibon the inner.

202

It is nowhere written that one should refrain from ceremonial worship of the gods in the tenth month, known as the Godless Month. There is no textual basis for the belief, but perhaps the month has this name because no shrine festivals are held during this month.

Some say that this is the month when all the gods gather at the Grand Shrine in Ise,[352] but there is no foundation for this. If it were the case, there should be special ceremonies held there in the tenth month, but this does not happen. There are numerous instances of imperial visits to shrines during this month, but most have been associated with inauspicious events.[353]

203

The custom of hanging a quiver on the gate of a house that has received an imperial reprimand is no longer extant, and no one now knows of it.

On occasions such as an imperial illness, or at times of general upheaval, a quiver is hung at Tenjin Shrine in Gojō. Yuki Shrine in the grounds of Kurama Temple[354] has likewise received a quiver as offering.

Once a police constable's quiver was placed on the gate of an imperially reprimanded household, no one could enter or leave. Now that this custom has lapsed, a seal is set there instead.

204

When a criminal is to be lashed with a cane, he is tied to a whipping post. It is said that no one any longer understands the correct form of the whipping post or the method of tying.

205

It was Abbot Jie who first wrote a document known as the Invocation and Vows to the Founder,[355] traditionally presented at the temple on Mount Hiei. Such documents are not dealt with in legal circles. Back in the days of the great emperors, they were never used for government purposes, but these days this has become common practice.

Furthermore, water and fire are not held to be polluted in the eyes of the law, although containers are.[356]

206

When the now-deceased Tokudaiji Minister of the Right[357] was Superintendent of Police, he was one day holding court at his central gate[358] when the ox of one of the officers, Akikane, broke loose, got into the court room, scrambled up on to the Superintendent's seating platform and there settled down to chew its cud. This was deemed a disturbingly untoward event, and everyone present declared that the beast should be taken off for Yin-Yang divination to determine the meaning.

However, when the Superintendent's father the Minister[359] heard of this, he declared, 'An ox has no understanding. It has its four legs which can take it anywhere. There is no reason to impound a skinny beast that happens to have brought some lowly official here.' He had the ox returned to its master, and changed the matting where the ox had lain. There were no ill consequences from the event.

It is sometimes said that if you see something sinister and choose to treat it as normal, you will thereby avert whatever it portended.

207

When the ground was being turned for the construction of the Kameyama Residence,[360] a mound was discovered that seethed with countless huge snakes. In the report to the retired emperor, they were described as the gods of the area. He sought advice on what should be done about them, and everyone declared that, since the snakes had always lived there, it would be a bad idea simply to destroy the mound and get rid of them.

This Minister[361] alone differed. 'Why should these creatures prove vengeful at the construction of an imperial residence, when they've been living all this time on imperial ground?' he said. '"Gods do no evil", after all. There's no need to worry about them. We should just go ahead and root them all out.'

So they did, and threw all the snakes into the nearby Ōi River. And no ill came of it.

208

Wrapping and tying off the cord of a sutra scroll involves crossing upper cord over lower, then drawing the loop at the end of the cord sideways through the crossed point. This is the normal method.

But Abbot Kōshun of Kegon-in Temple[362] undid cord tied in this way and retied it. 'That's the way people tie it these days,' he explained. 'It's dreadful. The proper way is simply to wrap the cord round and round, then tuck the ends in through the top.'

He was an elderly man, and well versed in the old ways.

209

A man who had lost his case for ownership of another's field, from sheer rage sent some men to plunder the field. As they went, they paused to ravage the other fields along the way. When challenged that these fields hadn't been at issue and asked why they had done this, they replied, 'Well there was no justification for cutting the rice in the other field either, so since we were out to make mischief why shouldn't we do a thorough job?'

What very odd reasoning.

210

All we know about the *yobukodori*[363] is that it is said to be a bird of spring. No record makes clear just what bird it is. One Shingon text gives instructions for a soul-returning ceremony[364] to be performed when the *yobukodori* sings. In this case, the reference is to a *nue*, or ground thrush.[365] The *nue* appears in the *Manyōshū chōka* poem[366] that begins 'The misty, long spring day . . .', suggesting that the *yobukodori* may well be similar to the ground thrush.

211

Nothing in this world can be trusted. Fools put all their faith in things, and so become angry and bitter.

The powerful should place no faith in their powerful position. The strong are the first to go. The rich should never depend on their wealth. A fortune can easily disappear from one moment to the next. A scholar should never be complacent about his skills. Even Confucius did not meet with the reception he deserved. The virtuous should not rely on their virtue. Even the exemplary Yan Hui met with misfortune.[367] Nor should those favoured by the emperor be smug. You may at any time find yourself instead faced with execution for some crime. Never rely on your servants to be loyal. They can rebel and flee. Never put your faith in others' goodwill. They will inevitably change their minds. Never depend on a promise made. People seldom keep their word.

If you rely neither on yourself nor on others, you will rejoice when things go well, and not be aggrieved when they don't. Maintain a clear space on either side, and nothing will obstruct you; keep open before and behind you, and you will be unimpeded. If you let yourself be hemmed in, you can be squeezed to breaking point. Without care and flexibility in your dealings with the world, you will find yourself in conflict and be damaged, while if you live calmly and serenely, not a hair on your head will come to harm.

Humans are the most miraculous and exalted of all things in heaven and earth.[368] And heaven and earth are boundless. How, then, could we differ in essence? If our spirit is open and boundless, neither fear nor joy will obstruct it, and we will remain untroubled by the world.

212

The moon of autumn is especially splendid. It is a sorry man indeed who cannot understand this distinction, and claims that it is no different from the moon at other seasons.

213

When lighting the charcoal in the imperial braziers, one never uses the normal metal chopsticks to transfer the lit coal. It should be put in directly from the earthenware vessel it is carried in. For this reason, the charcoal in the brazier should be heaped with great care, to prevent the lit coal from falling.[369]

When a white-clad retainer in an imperial progress to Yahata Shrine[370] was observed placing the charcoal by hand, someone versed in such matters declared that on days when one was dressed in white it was permissible to use metal chopsticks.

214

The name of the musical piece 'Sōfuren' does not in fact refer to the love of a wife for her husband, as suggested by the way it is written. It was originally written with different characters.[371] It is a piece depicting the pleasure that Wang Jian of the Jin dynasty[372] took in the lotuses he had planted at his home as Minister. This is why that office is euphemistically referred to as 'Lotus Mansion'.

In the same way, the piece titled 'Kaikotsu' should in fact be written with different characters that form the name of the Chinese land known to us as Kaikotsu,[373] a powerful barbarian realm. Once these barbarians had surrendered to the Han, they came to the capital, where they played their own music – hence the name of this piece.

215

When Lord Taira no Nobutoki[374] was old, he told the following story of former times.

'One evening, the Saimyōji Novice[375] summoned me. I replied that I would be there right away, but I didn't have a decent court robe, and while I was fussing around trying to organize one the messenger returned.

'"Perhaps you don't have the correct clothing?" said his message. "It is night, so there is no need to dress properly. Just come promptly." So I set off dressed as normal, in a shabby, unstarched robe.

'He produced a sake bottle and earthenware cups. "It would be depressing to drink this on my own," he said, "so I called you over. I'm afraid there are no snacks to have with it, and I should think everyone is sound asleep by now. Please go off and look around to see if you can find something suitable."

'I lit a taper and looked everywhere, till on one of the kitchen shelves I found a little earthenware plate with a smear of *miso* on it.

'"Here's what I could find," I told him.

'"That should do nicely," he replied, and set about merrily tossing back the sake, in fine spirits.

'That's how it was back in the old days,' Nobutoki finished.

216

Once, when the Saimyōji Novice was on pilgrimage to the Hachiman Shrine in Tsurugaoka,[376] he called on the home of the Ashikaga Sama Novice,[377] having sent an advance messenger. The novice entertained him on this occasion by producing with the first round of sake a dish of dried abalone strips, with the second prawns, and with the third and final round, rice cakes. Present at the time were the host and his wife, and Abbot Ryūben.[378]

The Saimyōji Novice mentioned that he was anxious to see the dyed Ashikaga cloth[379] that he received as a gift from his companion every year.

'I have it ready,' his host replied, and he produced thirty bolts of variously dyed cloth, which he had his ladies sew up into short-sleeved kimono before the Saimyōji Novice's very eyes, and afterwards presented to him.

All this I was told by someone who died only recently, who had personally witnessed it.

217

Here is what a very rich man once said to me:

'People should put all other things aside and devote themselves single-mindedly to acquiring wealth. There is no point in living if you're poor. Only the rich are worthy of the name "human".

'To gain wealth, you should first cultivate the right spirit. And what spirit might that be? Why, the firm belief that the human world is immutable, and never so much as a moment's pause to consider impermanence. This is the most important thing.

'Next, you must not attend to life's various demands. In this world of ours, there is no end to our own and others' wants. If you follow your desires in what you set out to attain, all your money will be gone before you know it, no matter how much you may have. Desire is limitless, while money is finite. You cannot use limited resources to fulfil unlimited craving. You must be immensely wary of indulging even the smallest urge, and treat any desire that might rear its head as a wicked impulse that is bound to ruin you.

'Next, be aware that if you treat your money like a mere servant, you will very soon find yourself in dire straits. You must venerate it like a revered master, worship it like a god and never bend it to your will. Next, avoid anger and bitterness if you meet with embarrassments in life. Next, always be honest, and honour all promises. For those who follow these rules in seeking wealth, riches will come as inevitably as fire catches dried wood or water flows downhill. Once you have stockpiled unlimited wealth, your desires – for banqueting, music, beautiful women, a finely appointed house – may go unmet, but you will always feel fulfilled and at peace,' he said.

People do indeed seek wealth in order to fulfil their desires. Money is seen as riches because it allows one to gain what one covets. Someone who has desire but does not fulfil it, who has money but does not use it, is essentially no different from a poor man. What might such a person find pleasure in? This man's teaching can be seen as an admonishment to relinquish worldly desires and not lament poverty. Far better, surely, not to have wealth than to find your pleasure in attaining your desires. Far better to avoid contracting boils and pustules in the first place than to find your pleasure in bathing them.

Once you have attained this state, there is no distinction between wealth and poverty. Enlightenment and delusion are one in Buddhist teaching. Great desire and desirelessness have much in common.

218

Foxes will bite people.

A retainer at the Horikawa Mansion[380] was once bitten on the foot by a fox while he slept. And one night, three foxes leaped out and bit a junior monk who was passing the main hall of Ninnaji Temple. He drew his sword and defended himself, managing to cut down two of them. One fox was killed, the other two escaped. The monk was bitten all over, but came to no real harm.

219

According to the Shijō Counsellor,[381] Tatsuaki[382] is a marvellous musician. He came to call on me the other day, and told me that he harboured some private doubts about the fifth hole of the transverse flute,[383] 'Although,' he added, 'I know virtually nothing of the instrument, so have deep hesitation in saying so.'

He went on to explain that the scale known as *hyōjō* is built on the second or *kan* hole, while that called *shimomujō* is built on the fifth hole. Between them lies the scale called *shōzetsujō*. The hole above this provides the *sōjō* scale, then on the *saku* hole above we find the *ōshikijō*, with the *fushōjō* between these two. Proceeding on up the flute, we have the intermediate, *rankeijō*, then the *banshikijō* built on the next or *chū* hole, and between this and the sixth hole lies the *shinsenjō* scale. Between each hole, in other words, we discover a scale. However, between the fifth and the one above it there is no intermediate scale. What's more, the distance between them is the same as for the other holes, which creates an unpleasant-sounding interval. For this reason, when covering the fifth hole the player will always lift his mouth a little from the embouchure. If he fails to do this, it creates a dissonance with the other instruments. 'Few players can manage this successfully,' he finished.

This was a most thoughtful and intriguing opinion, the Shijō Counsellor added, and a fine example of the old adage of the master being awed by one who comes after.[384]

On another occasion, though, Kagemochi[385] told me, 'The *shō*[386] is already perfectly tuned when you take it in your hands, so you need only blow. In the case of the transverse flute, however, you control the tuning with your breath as you blow, so every note, not only the fifth, requires the diligent attention of the player's own musical sense, as well as the instructions of tradition. One can't simply make the sweeping statement that you should lift your lips at the fifth hole – poor control will create a bad note at any hole, while good players can tune the notes produced from them all. It is the fault of the player, not the instrument, if the melody seems ill-matched to it.'

220

I once remarked that the *bugaku* performed at Tennōji Temple[387] is the sole exception to the rule that all things provincial are coarse and inferior, for it stands comparison with that of the capital.

A Tennōji musician replied that the music at his temple was finer than elsewhere because the pitch was carefully set and the instruments beautifully tuned. The temple takes its pitch from the bell that hangs before the Rokuji Hall, preserved from the time of the great Prince Shōtoku.[388] The tone of this bell gives the tone for the *ōshiki* mode.[389] Heat and cold would raise and lower it a little, so the tone produced between the Nehan and the Shōryō ceremonies[390] in the second month is used as the standard pitch. These are the secret teachings of the Tennōji *bugaku*.

'All our instruments are tuned from this single standard pitch,' he said.

As a general rule, a temple bell should be pitched to the *ōshiki*, a tone that resonates with a sense of impermanence or *mujō*, the note struck long ago by the bell of the Mujō Hall of Gion Shōja.[391] The bell at Saionji Temple[392] is said to have been recast numerous times in an attempt to tune it to this pitch, but to no avail, so a properly pitched bell was sought out from distant parts instead. The bell of Jōkongō-in[393] is also pitched to the *ōshiki*.

221

Elderly fourth-rank constabulary scholars[394] still tell of the time, back in the Kenji and Kōan eras,[395] when the constabulary guards in the festival procession[396] used to walk down the road chanting the contents of an old song, with, attached to their simple spider-web pattern *suikan* robe,[397] a horse constructed out of four or five lengths of peculiar dark-blue cloth, the mane and tail made of rush wicks. According to these men, everyone greatly enjoyed the sight of them at each festival.

These days, the decorations they wear for the festival are becoming more extravagant by the year. They pant along, weighed down with all manner of heavy objects, someone supporting the sleeves on either side, and don't even hold their own halberds. It is quite painful to behold.

222

Once when the monk Jōganbō of Takedani was visiting Tōnijō no In,[398] that lady enquired what rites were particularly effective in praying for the soul of the deceased.

'The Kōmyō Shingon and the Hōkyōin Darani,'[399] he replied.

His disciples asked him later why he had said this. 'Why didn't you tell her that nothing could be more effective than the *nenbutsu*?' they said.

'Indeed I would have liked to tell her this, since it is the teaching of our sect,' Jōganbō replied, 'but I've never seen it stated in any of the texts that chanting the name of Amida is effective in praying for the dead. If her ladyship had gone on to ask me for a reference to justify my claim I would have been hard put for a reply, so I decided to give her an answer with scriptural foundation. That is why I gave these two names.'

223

The Tazu Minister's[400] childhood name was Tazugimi. 'Tazu' is written with the character for 'crane', but the story that he acquired the name because he once reared cranes is mistaken.

224

The novice and Yin-Yang master Arimune[401] once sought me out when he had come up from Kamakura.

As soon as he came in, he said reprovingly, 'This garden is far too large – it's dreadful. People of real understanding put their energy into growing useful plants. You must turn all this into vegetable plots with a single narrow path between.'

It's quite true: it is a pointless waste to leave even the tiniest patch of land uncultivated. One should plant food or medicinal plants.

225

Ō no Hisasuke once told of how the novice Michinori chose certain particularly interesting dance moves, taught them to a dancer by the name of Iso no Zenji[402] and got her to dance them. She performed dressed in a white *suikan* robe, with a short sword at her side and a lacquered court cap on her head, so her dancing style was generally referred to as 'male'.

Her daughter Shizuka carried on this style. This was the beginning of the *shirabyōshi*,[403] which involves singing of the origins of the gods and buddhas. Minamoto no Mitsuyuki[404] later created many more songs, and there are also some composed by Retired Emperor Gotoba, who apparently taught them to the dancer Kamegiku.[405]

226

Back in the days of Retired Emperor Gotoba,[406] there was a former provincial governor of Shinano called Yukinaga,[407] who was famed for his learning. When summoned to the imperial presence to take part in a discussion on the *yuefu*,[408] he forgot two of the virtues in the poem 'Dance of the Seven Virtues'.[409] This earned him the nickname 'Young Master Five Virtues',[410] which so upset him that he abandoned scholarship and took the tonsure. The monk Jichin,[411] who treated kindly anyone with any artistic skill and took them into service, no matter how lowly, looked after him thereafter.

This novice Yukinaga created *The Tale of the Heike*, which he taught to the blind reciter Shōbutsu.[412] This is why that work goes into particular detail about Enryakuji.[413] Yoshitsune, the Kurō Lieutenant,[414] plays a prominent role owing to Yukinaga's detailed knowledge of him; the sketchy treatment of Noriyori, or Kaba no Kanja,[415] is probably because Yukinaga knew little about him. Being from the East, Shōbutsu gained information about warriors and martial matters from military men there, and passed on his knowledge to Yukinaga, who wrote it into the *Tale*. Present-day *biwa* reciters of the *Tale*[416] still imitate Shōbutsu's native pronunciation.

227

The Six Hour Praises was put together from an assemblage of sacred texts by Anraku, a disciple of the holy man Hōnen,[417] for use as a service. Later, an Uzumasa monk named Zenkanbō[418] added musical notations to give them the form of sung hymns. It was the beginning of the One Thought *nenbutsu*,[419] and began during the time of Retired Emperor Gosaga.[420] Zenkanbō was also the originator of the Service Hymn.[421]

228

The Senbon *shaka nenbutsu* was begun by the holy priest Nyorin in the Bun'ei period.[422]

229

It is said that good carving should be performed with a slightly blunt blade. Myōken's[423] blade cut very poorly.

230

The Gojō Palace[424] was haunted.

The Tō Grand Counsellor[425] related how one day when the senior courtiers were playing *go* in the Black Door room, something raised the blind.

'Who's there?' they said, and turned to see a fox[426] kneeling there, just like a person, peering in. 'Hey, it's a fox!' everyone yelled, whereupon it fled in panic.

Perhaps it was a fox that hadn't yet learned how to transform itself properly.

231

The Superintendent Novice Sono[427] was a master of cuisine. A marvellous carp was once presented at a certain household. Everyone present was longing to see how Novice Sono would handle it, but hesitated simply to ask him.

Being the man he was, however, he understood the situation. 'I've been practising my knife skills on carp for a hundred days,' he said, 'so today must be no exception. I humbly request that I be allowed to work on this carp,' and, so saying, he sliced it up. This was perfect for the occasion, and everyone was most amused.

When someone related this to the Kitayama Minister Novice,[428] however, he remarked, 'Personally, I find that very irritating. He would have done better to say, "If there's no one else who can cut it up, let me do it." Why bring up the matter of the hundred days like that?'

Someone told me this tale because they found it amusing, and I did too.

On the whole, it is better to do something unimpressively and simply rather than strive for effect. It is certainly a fine thing to make sure your guests' banquet is all it should be, but it is also excellent to simply present the meal without fuss. Similarly with giving a gift – the more sincere gesture is simply to say, 'Here's something for you,' rather than present it on a special occasion. It is unpleasant behaviour to give a gift with apparent reluctance, or make it seem some kind of reward from loser to winner.

232

As a rule, people should display no learning or art.

I remember someone's son, a not unattractive youth, who would quote from *The Histories*[429] when talking to others in his father's presence. He came across as very clever, certainly, but one did wish he wouldn't behave in this manner before his betters.

On another occasion, the host called for a *biwa* to be produced so that the gathering could hear a recitation. When it arrived, one of the bridges was found to be missing, so he ordered a new one to be made. One of those present, a man who seemed quite well bred, asked if there was an old wooden ladle whose handle could be used.[430] I looked at his hands and noted that he had the long nails of a *biwa* player. But the *biwa* was only for use by a blind reciter on this occasion, so there was no need for such finesse.[431] I decided he must be simply flaunting his expertise, and I was quite put off. Someone later pointed out that a ladle's handle is made of the kind of wood used for containers,[432] so was unsuitable.

The slightest thing can show up a young person in either a good or a bad light.

233

If you wish to be free of fault in all matters, be sincere in whatever you do, polite to all, and speak little. Beauty of speech leaves a beguiling and unforgettable impression; this holds for everyone, man or woman, young or old, but particularly for the young and attractive.

All faults derive from making oneself out to be expert and at ease with things, being smug, and despising others.

234

Some will give a confusingly vague response to a question, perhaps in the belief that the enquirer must really know the answer already so they would look silly to provide a straight explanation. This is not the way to behave. Even if he does know, he may wish to clarify the matter – and surely it is possible that someone genuinely does not know. You will seem more sensible if you give a straightforward response.

If you send a message along the lines of 'Isn't that business about so-and-so astonishing?' referring to something you happen to know but the other has not yet heard of, he must send back to ask what you are talking about, which is very annoying and unpleasant for him. It is always possible that someone hasn't heard about it, even if it is old news for everyone else. What could be wrong with making clear what you are talking about?

Such behaviour is typical of the immature.

235

People do not simply take it into their heads to walk into some house if the owner is present. But if a house is empty, passers-by will casually come in, the lack of human presence will encourage foxes and owls to make themselves at home there, and tree spirits and suchlike bizarre creatures will even appear.

Likewise, since a mirror has no inherent shape or colour, everything can appear reflected in it. If it had its own colour and shape, it wouldn't reflect other things.

The emptiness of space allows it to contain things. The fact that thoughts can come crowding into our mind at will must mean that 'mind' is actually an empty space too. If someone were really in residence there, it would surely not be invaded by all these thoughts.

236

There is a place in Tamba[433] called Izumo, where the deity of the great Izumo Shrine has been installed[434] in a magnificent shrine building. The area is ruled by a certain Shida,[435] who one autumn invited a great many people, including the holy man Shōkai.[436] 'Come and pray to Izumo,' he said, 'and let us feast on rice cakes.' He led them to the shrine, and every one of them prayed and was filled with faith.

The holy man was immensely moved by the sight of the guardian Chinese lion and Korean dog,[437] which were placed back to back and facing backwards. 'How marvellous!' he exclaimed, close to tears. 'Such an unusual position to stand them in! There must be some deep reason behind it.' Then he turned to the others. 'How can you not have noticed this wonder?' he cried. 'I'm amazed at you.'

They were very struck. 'Yes indeed,' they all declared, 'they *are* different from elsewhere. We'll tell this to everyone back in the capital.'

The holy man now wished to learn more, so he called over an elderly and wise-looking shrine priest. 'There must be some interesting tale explaining the placement of these images,' he said. 'Do be so kind as to tell us.'

'Indeed there is,' replied the priest. 'Some naughty children did it. A disgraceful business,' and so saying he went over to the statues, set them to rights and walked off.

The holy man's tears of delight had been for nothing.

237

Perhaps the vertical or horizontal placement of objects on a willow-work stand[438] depends on the object. The Sanjō Minister of the Right[439] once told me that scrolls and so forth should be placed vertically and tied in place with a twist of paper passed between the slats, and an ink stone should likewise be vertical, since this prevents the brushes rolling off.

The great calligraphers of the Kadenokōji house,[440] however, never placed it lengthwise, even temporarily. It was always horizontal.

238

The imperial guard Chikatomo[441] once drew up a list of seven things in his own praise. They were all to do with the art of horsemanship, and not particularly impressive. This precedent encourages me to make my own list of seven.

1. I was out viewing the blossoms one day with a large group of companions when we came cross a man galloping his horse in the vicinity of Saishōkō-in.[442] 'If he does that again,' I predicted, 'the horse will fall and he will come off. Wait and see.' We paused to watch. Sure enough, he set his horse galloping again, and as he pulled up the horse was dragged over, and the rider tumbled into the mud. Everyone was most impressed that my prediction had proven right.

2. When our present emperor[443] was still crown prince, his palace was in Madenokōji. I once had occasion to call in on the chamber occupied by the Horikawa Grand Counsellor[444] when in attendance, and found him with the scrolls of books four, five and six of the *Analects* spread before him. 'His Highness wanted to look at the passage about Confucius hating to see purple trumping red,'[445] he said, 'but he was unable to locate it. He has asked me to continue the search.'

'You'll find it in such-and-such a place in the ninth scroll,' I told him.

He was delighted, and carried it off to show His Highness.

This is the kind of thing even children can usually manage, but in the old days people used to praise themselves to the skies about even trivial achievements.

When Retired Emperor Gotoba asked Lord Teika[446] whether it was permissible to use the two words for sleeve, *sode* and *tamoto*,[447] in the same poem, Teika replied, 'It is perfectly fine. We have the precedent of the old poem[448]

Are the *susuki* grasses	*aki no no no*
the *sleeves* of the autumn fields?	*kusa no* tamoto *ka*
For their fluttering heads	*hanasuzuki*
seem like yearning *sleeves*	*ho ni idete maneku*
waving and beckoning	sode *to miyuran*

Teika writes of this very pretentiously,[449] describing how he recalled the poem at this critical moment and claiming that it showed his great good fortune in being under the special protection of the god of poetry. There is similar boasting of the most trifling things in the request for promotion submitted by the Kujō Chief Minister Koremichi.[450]

3. The inscription on the bell of Jōzaikō-in Temple is in the hand of Lord Arikane.[451] Lord Yukifusa[452] made a fair copy, and when this was to be transferred to the mould for the bell, the novice in charge took out the copy and showed it to me. It contained the lines, 'Beyond the flowers the tolling bell sends off the darkening evening. / Its sound is heard a hundred miles away.'[453]

'This looks as if it was composed in the Yangtang scheme,'[454] I said, 'in which case I suspect "a hundred miles" is likely to be a mistake.'

'I'm very glad I showed you,' he said. 'A very wise thing to do.' He passed on my opinion to Lord Arikane, who replied that there was indeed a mistake, and 'a hundred miles' should be changed to 'some leagues'. I'm not sure about 'some leagues' either. It is possible that it should be 'some furlongs'.[455]

('Some leagues' is indeed suspicious.[456] 'Some' means at most four or five, but there is nothing impressive in a bell being heard four or five furlongs away. The phrase simply means that the bell was heard far away.)

4. I once went with a large group of people on the Three Pagodas Pilgrimage,[457] and in the Jōgyō Hall at Yokawa we saw an old piece of framed calligraphy with the inscription 'Ryōge-in'.[458] The priest of the temple solemnly explained that there was an unresolved debate over whether it was by Sari or Kōzei.[459] 'If it's by Kōzei,' I said, 'there will be a signature on the reverse. If by Sari, then not.' The back was filthy, a nest for insects and smothered in dust, but we carefully wiped it clean and all saw clearly written there the name 'Kōzei', with his rank and the date. Everyone was most impressed.

5. Once, when the holy priest Dōgen was giving a lecture at Narandaji Temple, he forgot what the Eight Calamities[460] consist of.

'Can anyone remember them?' he asked, but none of the listening monks could.

I spoke up from where I sat beyond the screen,[461] 'Would they be . . . ?' I suggested, and proceeded to list them. Everyone was full of admiration.

6. I had accompanied Abbot Kenjō to see the Perfumed Water Purification.[462] The Abbot left before the ceremony was over, but the monk who had accompanied him was nowhere to be seen. The monks were sent back in to search for him, but they emerged after a long time, declaring there were so many others all looking much the same that it was impossible to find him. 'Oh dear, oh dear,' said the Abbot, turning to me. 'Could you look for him?' So I went back inside and very soon emerged with the man.

7. On the fifteenth day of the second month, a bright moonlit night, I went very late to the Senbon Temple.[463] I entered from behind the crowd of worshippers and was sitting there quietly, face deeply hidden, listening to the ceremony, when a lady of unusually refined fragrance and appearance made her way through the people and came and kneeled right beside me, close enough for her scent to pervade me. 'This is rather awkward,' I thought, and I shifted away a little on my knees, but she edged closer again until we were as before. At this point I rose and left.

Later, an elderly gentlewoman at a refined establishment was chatting idly of this and that when she mentioned that she had once had occasion to look down on me as a very ungallant fellow. 'There's a lady who considers you a horribly cold fish,' she told me. I replied that I had no idea what she was talking about, and that was that.

But I subsequently heard that that night at the temple a fine lady had spied me from where she was seated behind her screen. She spruced up her gentlewoman prettily and sent her off to me. 'With luck,' she said, 'you'll be able to speak to him. Come back and tell me what he was like. This should be fun.' It had apparently all been planned.

239

The fifteenth day of the eighth month and the thirteenth day of the ninth month are both *rōshuku* days[464] in the celestial calendar. This constellation being clear and bright, these are particularly good nights for enjoying the moon.

240

He whose deep love spurs him to dare all and go to his beloved, though 'watchful eyes surround the stealthy lover' and 'guards are set to snare him in the dark',[465] will leave them both replete with powerful memories of all the moments when they tasted life's poignancy to the full. It must feel very awkward and unromantic for the woman, however, if a man simply takes her as his wife with the full consent of the family and without further ado.

How dreary it is when a woman hard up in the world announces that she will 'answer the call of any current'[466] so long as he is well-off, be it some unsuitable old priest or an uncouth Easterner, and a go-between sets about singing the praises of each to the other, with the result that she comes to someone's house as a bride without either knowing the other at all. What on earth would they say to each when they first come face to face? On the other hand, a couple can find endless conversation in the memories of long hardships overcome, 'forging their way through the dense autumn woods'[467] to be together at last.

It can generally be said that a great deal of dissatisfaction results from a marriage set up by a third party. If the wife is excellent and the man a lowly and ugly old fellow, he will despise her for allowing herself to be thrown away on the likes of himself, and feel ashamed in her presence – a deplorable situation.

If you can never linger beneath the clouded moon on a plum-scented evening, nor find yourself recalling the dawns when you made your way home through the dew-soaked grasses by her gate after a night of love, you had best not aspire to be a lover at all.

241

The full moon's perfect roundness lasts barely a moment, and in no time is lost. Those with no eye for such things, it seems, fail to see how it changes in the course of a night.

An illness will grow graver as each moment passes, and death is already close at hand, yet while the sickness is still mild and you are not yet confronting death, you are lulled by your accustomed assumptions of a normal life in an unchanging world, and choose to wait until you have accomplished all you want in life before calmly turning your thoughts to salvation and a Buddhist practice, with the result that when you fall ill and confront death, none of your dreams has been fulfilled. Now, too late, you repent of your long years of negligence, and swear that if only you were to recover you would dedicate yourself unstintingly day and night to this thing and that – but for all your prayers your illness grows graver, until you lose your senses and die a raving death. It happens to so many of us. We must fully grasp this, here and now.

If you plan to turn your thoughts to the Buddhist Way after you have fulfilled all your desires, you will find that those desires are endless. What could be achieved, in this illusory life of ours? All desire is delusion. If desires arise within you, realize that they spring from your lost and deluded mind, and ignore them all. Relinquish all today and turn to the Buddhist path, and you will be freed of all obstruction, released from the need for action, and lasting peace will be yours body and soul.

242

We are forever ruled by the joys and sorrows of circumstance thanks to our preoccupation with pleasure and pain. Pleasure means fondness and love. These we ceaselessly pursue. Firstly, we pursue fame. This is of two kinds – renown for our conduct, and renown for our skill. Second is lust. Third is appetite. All other desires are secondary to these three.

These desires arise from mistaken understanding, and are the cause of much suffering. It is best to have nothing to do with them.

243

The year I turned eight, I asked my father, 'What sort of thing is a buddha?'

'A buddha is what a human becomes,'[468] he replied.

'How does a human become a buddha?' I asked.

'You become a buddha by following the Buddha's teaching,' he answered.

'So who taught the Buddha?' I asked.

'He became a buddha by following the teaching of previous buddhas,' he said.

'So what sort of buddha was the first one who began the teaching?' I asked.

My father laughed and replied, 'I suppose he just fell from the sky like rain or rose out of the earth like water.'

He used to enjoy recounting this story to others, adding, 'He had me cornered. I couldn't think what to reply.'

Map

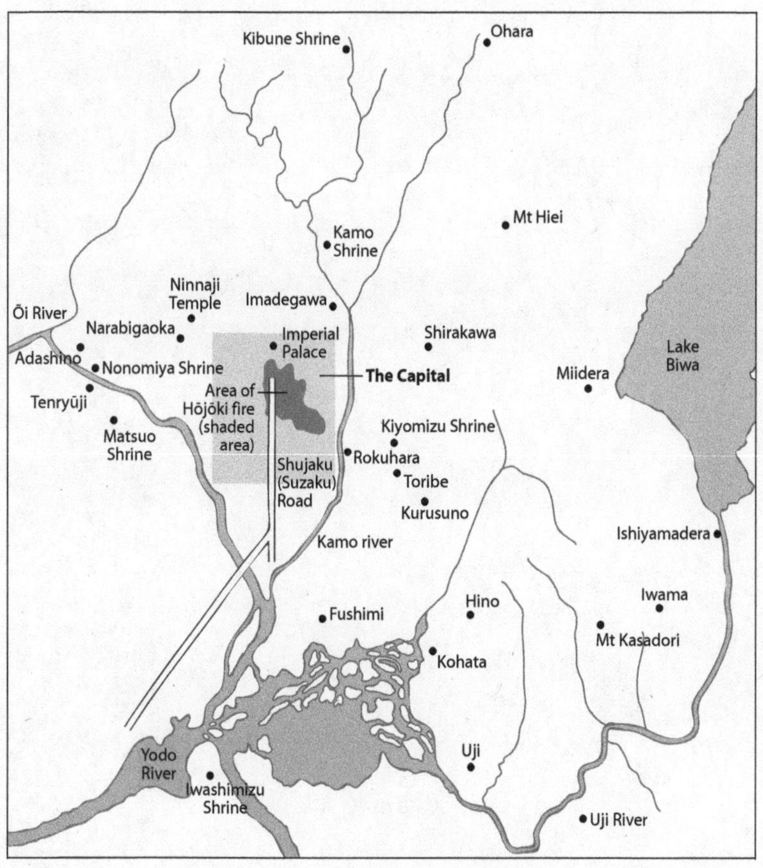

Kibune Shrine
Ohara
Mt Hiei
Kamo
Shrine
Ninnaji
Temple
Imadegawa
Ōi River
Narabigaoka
Imperial
Palace
Shirakawa
Adashino
Nonomiya Shrine
The Capital
Lake
Biwa
Miidera
Area of
Hōjōki fire
(shaded
area)
Tenryūji
Matsuo
Shrine
Kiyomizu Shrine
Rokuhara
Shujaku
(Suzaku)
Road
Toribe
Kurusuno
Ishiyamadera
Kamo river
Iwama
Hino
Fushimi
Mt Kasadori
Kohata
Uji
Yodo
River
Iwashimizu
Shrine
Uji River

Timeline of Emperors

This list gives the names and relevant details of the emperors mentioned in the text. From the abdication of Shirakawa in 1086 until the reign of Godaigo 235 years later, effective power resided with the retired emperors, who governed as regents for the usually very young and powerless emperors who reigned during their lifetime.

SAIMEI 594–661. Reigned 655–61.

SAGA 786–842. Reigned 809–23.

KŌKŌ 830–87. Reigned 884–7.

DAIGO 885–930. Reigned 897–930.

MURAKAMI 926–67. Reigned 946–67.

SHIRAKAWA 1053–1129. Reigned 1072–86. After his abdication he took the tonsure but continued to exercise power during the reigns of the three subsequent emperors, effectively instituting the Insei, or rule from retirement, system.

HORIKAWA 1079–1107. Reigned 1086–1107. Son of Shirakawa, who as retired emperor held the power during his reign.

TOBA 1103–56. Reigned 1107–23. At the death of his grandfather, Shirakawa, in 1129 he gained effective power as retired emperor. Having set his son Sutoku, on the throne, he later forced him to abdicate in favour of a later son Konoe, on whose death he placed another son Goshirakawa, on the throne, thereby helping to instigate the devastating wars between the Genji and the Heike clans (see Introduction).

SUTOKU 1119–64. Reigned 1123–41. His reign was dominated by his grandfather (Shirakawa) and later his father (Toba), who forced his abdication in favour of a later son (Konoe, 1139–55, r. 1141–55). When Goshirakawa was placed on the throne at Konoe's death, Sutoku unsuccessfully attempted to seize the throne with the aid of factions at court, but was defeated and exiled to Sanuki (present-day Shikoku), where he remained until his death.

GOSHIRAKAWA 1127–92. Reigned 1155–8. Son of Toba. After abdicating in favour of his son Nijō (1143–65, r. 1158–65), he continued effectively to govern from retirement during the reigns of Nijō, Rokujō (1164–76, r. 1165–8), Takakura, Antoku (1178–85, r. 1180–85) and Gotoba.

KAMO NO CHŌMEI, AUTHOR OF HŌJŌKI, BORN C.1155.

TAKAKURA 1161–81. Reigned 1168–80. Son of Goshirakawa. His reign was dominated by the rise of Taira no Kiyomori (see Introduction). He was succeeded by his infant son Antoku, who was drowned during the battle between the Heike and Genji clans at Dannoura.

GOTOBA 1180–1239. Reigned 1183–98. He came to the throne after his brother Antoku was swept up in the clan wars between the Heike and the Genji. After his abdication, he reigned as Cloistered Emperor until 1221, when an unsuccessful coup against the Hōjō led to his exile to Oki Island, where he remained until his death.

JUNTOKU 1197–1242. Reigned 1210–21. Son of Gotoba, whom he supported in his efforts to overthrow the Hōjō. Exiled to Sado Island 1221, where he remained until his death.

KAMO NO CHŌMEI DIED 1216.

GOSAGA 1220–72. Reigned 1242–6. After an early abdication, he effectively held power as retired emperor during the reigns of his two sons, Gofukakusa and Kameyama. He instigated the alternate rule of the two imperial lines descending from these two sons (see Introduction).

GOFUKAKUSA 1243–1304. Reigned 1246–59. Son of Gosaga, who effectively ruled during his reign. Abdicated in favour of his brother Kameyama, regaining influence during the reigns of his son Fushimi and grandson Gofushimi.

KAMEYAMA 1249–1305. Reigned 1259–74.

GOUDA 1267–1324. Reigned 1274–87. His reign was dominated by his retired father, Kameyama. He abdicated in favour of his cousin, Fushimi, gaining greater influence when his son Gonijō (1285–1308, r. 1301–8) later ascended the throne.

YOSHIDA KENKŌ, AUTHOR OF ESSAYS IN IDLENESS, BORN c.1283.

FUSHIMI 1265–1317. Reigned 1287–98. Son of Gofukakusa, who effectively ruled during his reign.

GOFUSHIMI 1288–1336. Reigned 1298–1301. Son of Fushimi. Gofukakusa effectively ruled during his reign. He was forced by Gouda to abdicate, and was replaced by Gouda's son Gonijō.

HANAZONO 1297–1348. Reigned 1308–18. Son of Fushimi and successor of Gonijō. His father was effective ruler during his reign. Abdicated in favour of Godaigo.

GODAIGO 1288–1339. Reigned 1318–39. Son of Gouda, who effectively ruled during his reign until 1321, when Godaigo abolished the system of rule from retirement and restored the power of the emperor. His urge for political reform led to conflict with the shogun. He was deposed in 1331 and exiled to the island of Oki, from which he escaped and regained the throne. A further defeat led him to retreat to Yoshino, where he continued to assert the legitimacy of his reign against the alternative imperial line (Emperor Kōmyō until his death).

KŌMYŌ 1321–80. Reigned 1336–48. Placed on the throne by the shogun (Ashikaga Takauji) when Godaigo fled to Yoshino, he represented the alternative 'northern' dynasty that continued for sixty years. He abdicated in favour of his nephew Sukō (1334–98, r. 1349–51). Both men were captured in 1351 by the army of the 'southern' dynasty emperor of the day, Gomurakami (1328–68, r. 1339–68) and held prisoner for six years.

YOSHIDA KENKŌ DIED c.1350.

Notes

HŌJŌKI

1. *the third year of Angen*: 1177.
2. *the Hour of the Dog*: 7 p.m.–9 p.m.
3. *the Shujaku Gate . . . and the Civil Affairs Bureau*: The Shujaku Gate was the central southern entrance gate to the imperial palace. The Hall of State (*daikokuden*) to its north was used for important ceremonies. The University Hall (*daigkuryō*) was a large building to the east of the gate, and the Civil Affairs Bureau (*minbushō*), south-east of the Hall of State, oversaw taxation, censuses and public works. The fire in fact consumed not only these buildings in the imperial palace precinct, but a large part of the city.
4. *the fourth year of Jishō*: 1180.
5. *Nakamikado Kyōgoku . . . Rokujō*: i.e. roughly southward over an area covering about a mile from the eastern edge of the city.
6. *gates*: A gate (*mon*) was often a substantial structure, with two or four strong pillars, a thatched roof and heavy wooden doors.
7. *cypress bark thatch and shingles*: The houses of nobles, and temples and shrines, were roofed with layered squares of cypress bark, while those of commoners used wooden slats.
8. *karmic wind*: (*Gōfū*) A wind that arises from human sin, and carries sinners to hell.
9. *the sixth month . . . the capital was suddenly relocated*: Kyoto briefly ceased to be the capital in 1180, when the ruler Taira no Kiyomori (1118–81) moved it to Fukuhara in Settsu (present-day Kobe). The sudden announcement caused great confusion and disruption.
10. *it was so designated in the time of Emperor Saga*: In fact, present-day Kyoto was designated the new capital less than 400 years earlier, in 794, by Emperor Kanmu.

11. *floated down the Yodo*: The timber, etc. was floated down the Kamo and Uji Rivers and thence down the Yodo River into Osaka Bay to the new capital, and the houses were reconstructed there.
12. *prized only the horse and saddle ... went quite unused*: The ox-drawn carriage had long been a sign of status, but now that flexibility and mobility were so important they became too cumbersome. A deeper shift of values, from the primacy of the old court-centred aristocracy to the emerging warrior class, is also implied.
13. *property on the south-west seaboard ... to the north or east*: Wealth for the upper classes was largely dependent on ownership of privately taxed estates. The areas of Kyushu in the west and Shikoku, Ki, etc. in the south were the traditional strongholds of the Heike family, whose political power had now reached its zenith.
14. *the area was too cramped ... steeply up to mountains*: Although these words are not found in the Daifukukōji text, they are included in all other texts, and are necessary to the structure of the sentence.
15. *the old Log Palace*: The palace of the early Emperor Saimei (594–661) was said to have been a primitive construction of uncut logs. It is referred to as the Log Palace in a poem by Emperor Tenchi (?625–71).
16. *the new hitatare*: The *hitatare* was the formal clothing favoured by the new warrior class, whom these courtiers were now beginning to ape.
17. *the Yōwa era*: The short ten-month reign of the infant Emperor Antoku, 1181–2.
18. *till the fields in spring*: This phrase, omitted in the Daifukukōji text, appears in all other versions, and provides necessary balance for the sentence.
19. *despaired*: This is one possible interpretation of a word whose meaning has yet to be clarified.
20. *the dry river bed*: The meandering Kamo River, which flowed along the eastern edge of the capital, created river flats that were used by beggars and as thoroughfares in the dry season.
21. *these vile latter days*: It was common belief that the world had entered the latter days of the Buddhist Law, a degenerate age when evil was rife.
22. *Ryūgyō Hōin from Ninnaji*: Dates unknown. The title Hōin indicates a high-ranking priest. Ninnaji Temple stood at the time on the northern edge of the capital.

23. *the sacred Sanskrit syllable 'A'*: The first syllable of the ancient Sanskrit alphabet, it was believed to be a manifestation of Mahāvairocana Buddha, with the power to extinguish all suffering.
24. *from Ichijō south . . . and Shujaku east*: I.e. the eastern, more populous, section of the city.
25. *the Kamo riverbed, Shirakawa and the Nishi no Kyō*: Kawara was the riverbank area of the Kamo River to the east, the village of Shirakawa lay north-east of this, and Nishi no Kyō was the dilapidated area west of Suzaku.
26. *back in the Chōshō era*: The Chōshō era (1132–5) covered part of the reign of Sutoku.
27. *around the same time, as I recall*: The earthquake occurred three years later, in 1185.
28. *four elements*: According to Buddhist doctrine, these are earth, water, fire and wind.
29. *the Saikō era*: 854–7.
30. *the buddha of Tōdaiji Temple*: The large statue of the Buddha housed in Tōdaiji Temple in Nara.
31. *add any decent outbuildings*: A man of status would live in a walled compound consisting of storehouse, stables, etc. besides the main dwelling.
32. *the carriage*: An ox-drawn cart, commonly used for transport. It would normally have been housed in a more substantial building.
33. *some thirty troubled years*: Calculated from the time his troubles began, rather than from his age.
34. *my fiftieth year . . . turned my back on the world*: Chōmei became a lay monk (see Introduction) in 1204. By Western calculation, he was forty-nine.
35. *I made my bed among the clouds of Ōhara's mountains*: The elegant image of 'lying among the clouds' was a trope from Chinese poetry, expressing the life of one who had forsaken society to live as a recluse in nature. Ōhara is a village to the north of the capital.
36. *at sixty*: A poetic exaggeration that serves to emphasize his extreme age at the time he moved to Hino. In fact, though old in current terms, he was only fifty-four.
37. *an offerings shelf at its western edge*: A shelf on which flowers and water are placed as Buddhist offerings. Amida's Pure Land paradise is located in the west.
38. *a painted image of Amida . . . a copy of The Lotus Sutra placed before them*: The bodhisattva Amida (Amitābha) promises

salvation in the Western Paradise of the Pure Land (*saihō jōdo*) to all who pray to him. Fugen (Samantabhadra) is the bodhisattva of wisdom and compassion. *The Lotus Sutra* (*Saddharmapundarīka-sūtra*) is a key text of Mahayana Buddhism. These three were popular objects of worship in the Buddhism of the period.

39. *the poetic anthologies . . . Essentials of Salvation*: The poetic anthologies would be the classic imperial collections such as *Kokinshū*. *Essentials of Salvation* (*Ōjō Yōshū*, 985), a key religious work of its time by the priest Genshin (942–1017), preaches on the sufferings of the world and salvation through recitation of the *nenbutsu*, the sacred name of Amida (see note 45 below).

40. *one koto and one biwa . . . detachable neck*: Two popular stringed instruments; the multi-stringed *koto* rests on the ground before the player, while the four- or five-stringed *biwa* (a form of lute) is strummed or plucked. The jointed versions of these instruments could be disassembled for easy transport.

41. *Toyama*: Literally 'outside mountain', a word meaning a hill or mountain close to human settlement, presumably applied to this mountain as a proper name by the nearby inhabitants. It was in the grounds of Hōkaiji Temple in the mountainous area of Hino, south-east of the capital.

42. *the purple clouds that bear the soul to heaven*: The souls of the newly dead were believed to be lifted to Amida's Pure Land on a purple cloud.

43. *the hototogisu . . . to lead me over the mountain path of death*: The *hototogisu*, a kind of cuckoo with a lilting call that sings in early summer, was believed in folklore to have intimate knowledge of the difficult mountain path that the soul must cross after death.

44. *a fleeting life so soon cast off*: *Utsusemi*, the cast-off skin of a cicada, has the alternative meaning of the ephemeral nature of our present body or existence. The cricket is likewise associated with transience, since its melancholy song is heard only for a short time in autumn before the cold kills it.

45. *nenbutsu*: The chanted form of the name of the bodhisattva Amitābha (Japanese Amida), believed to have the power to lead believers to rebirth in Amida's Pure Land.

46. *the evils of speech*: One of three types of karmic sin or evil, the others being sins of the mind and sins of the body.

47. *the precepts*: There were varying degrees of strictness to the precepts depending on one's position. As one who had formally 'left the world' but not joined a temple community as a monk, Chōmei would probably have undertaken to obey the novice's Ten Precepts, which included prohibitions on killing, drinking alcohol, lascivious living, etc.
48. *'white retreating waves' . . . Okanoya . . . Novice Mansei*: Mansei's (fl. 704–31) famous poem – 'To what shall I compare / this transient world we live in? / White retreating waves / behind a boat that vanishes / rowing into the light of dawn' – became a byword for the ephemeral nature of life. The sentence implies that, like Mansei, Chōmei is composing poetry on life's transiency. Okanoya was an area along the Uji River, not far from Hino.
49. *the katsura trees . . . Xunyang Inlet . . . Tsunenobu*: *Katsura* (*Cercidiphyllum japonicum*), a common tree in montane forests, presumably grew around his hut. Xunyang Inlet was reputedly where the popular Chinese poet Bai Juyi (Japanese Hakurakuten) heard a maiden plucking her *biwa* (Chinese *pipa*) and was moved to write *The Song of the Pipa*. The poem's opening lines mention the *katsura* tree. Minamoto no Tsunenobu (1016–97) was renowned for his skills in poetry and music.
50. *'Autumn Wind Music', or 'Flowing Spring'*: Classic pieces in the repertoire of the *koto* and *biwa* respectively.
51. *Mount Kohata . . . Hatsukashi*: The description moves progressively west from the foothills of Mount Hino. These and the following place names hold strong poetic associations.
52. *follow the ridgeline over Mount Sumi . . . Ishiyama Temples*: The route crosses two low mountains to the west of Hino, then branches south to Iwama Temple and north to the more distant Ishiyama Temple.
53. *the plain of Awazu . . . the grave of Sarumaro*: Awazu lay beyond Ishiyama Temple, between present-day Zeze and the Seta River on Lake Biwa. Semimaru was a semi-legendary poet and blind monk of the ninth century. No site relating to him has been identified in this area. Tanakami River's present name is Daito River. It flows into the Seta. Sarumaro (dates unknown) was a ninth-century poet whose grave was believed to be in the area.
54. *the moon at my window . . . the cries of the monkeys*: The wailing of the monkey's cry and the association of the moon with past friends are classic poetic conceits in Chinese poetry.

55. *the fishermen's fires of distant Makinoshima . . . treetops*: Fishermen lit fires along the shore to attract fish at night. Makinoshima was on the bank of the Uji River to the east. The image of waking to rain and hearing it as wind in the trees is a reference to a poem by Nōin (988–?).
56. *When I hear the soft cry of the pheasant . . . father or mother*: A reference to a poem by the monk Gyōki (668–749), expressing a Buddhist understanding of the karmic interconnectedness of life.
57. *vine fibre*: Fibre derived from the stem of the *kuzu* vine (*Pueraria lobata*) made a coarse cloth.
58. *wild asters*: The young leaves were eaten.
59. *The Triple World is solely Mind*: The Buddhist concept of the Triple World (*sankai*) – of desire, form and formlessness – conceives the world in terms of the graded realms of human rebirth. This statement expresses the doctrine of idealism (*yuishinron*), which sees the world as a product of the mind. This passage summarizes words found in various sutras.
60. *the Three Paths*: The hell realms into which the sinful sink at their death.
61. *the hut of the holy Vimilakîrti . . . Śuddhipanthaka*: Vimilakîrti, an idealized lay follower of the Buddha, was commonly portrayed as living in seclusion in a small 'ten-foot square' (*hōjō*) hut. Śuddhipanthaka was a disciple of the Buddha who achieved enlightenment despite his immense stupidity.
62. *three faltering invocations . . . name of Amida*: The name of Amida is chanted to attain salvation. The description of it here as 'unapproachable' (*fusei*, literally 'unable to be asked') is the subject of scholarly debate, but is interpreted here to imply that Chōmei feels himself unworthy to ask for salvation.
63. *the second year of Kenryaku, by the monk Ren'in*: 1212. Ren'in was the Buddhist name of Kamo no Chōmei.

ESSAYS IN IDLENESS

1. *having sprung from no mere human seed*: The imperial line was believed to have been of divine origin.
2. *the great ruler*: *Ichi no hito*, a term referring to the regent (*sesshō*), chancellor (*kanpaku*) or similar high position in the government hierarchy.

3. *attendant guards to serve them:* Nobles were granted the use of imperial guards of various kinds for their personal protection, the quota depending on rank.
4. *Sei Shōnagon*: (*c.*966–1017), gentlewoman in Empress Teishi's court. The quotation is from her *Pillow Book* (*Makura no sōshi*) (see the Introduction).
5. *the holy man Sōga*: (917–1003), a Tendai sect monk, renowned in legend for his miraculous powers, who chose to retreat to the mountains and pursue a solitary practice. These words appear as a song he was said to sing (*Hosshinshū* 1.5).
6. *A man should learn the orthodox literature*: The literature traditionally considered proper for a gentleman was the Confucian classics.
7. *carry the rhythm well . . . at banquets*: Generally thought to be a reference to the wooden clapsticks used to beat the rhythm at performances of courtly songs (*kagura* and *saibara*).
8. *the great emperors of old*: Emperors of earlier centuries, such as Daigo and Murakami, were held up as ideals of governance.
9. *the Kujō Minister of the Right . . . his Precepts*: Fujiwara Morosuke (908–60). *Precepts* detailed his thoughts on proper court conduct.
10. *'The emperor should clothe himself simply'*: These words are found in *Kimpishō* (1218–21).
11. *a beautiful wine cup that lacks a base*: This quote is from *Wenxuan* 2:3, a Chinese collection of miscellaneous writings from down the centuries, influential among Japan's littérateurs. Kenkō's ideal of the lover derives from an earlier courtly ideal embodied in famous literary heroes such as Ariwara no Narihira (*The Tales of Ise*) and Hikaru Genji (*The Tale of Genji*).
12. *Counsellor Akimoto*: (1000–1047), a favourite of the emperor of the time, he took the tonsure when the emperor died, and became renowned as a hermit-aesthete. His story appears in a number of earlier sources, which often depict him speaking these words while plucking a lute.
13. *Prince Kaneakira, the Kujō Chief Minister and the Hanazono Minister of the Left*: Prince Kaneakira (914–87), Fujiwara Nobunaga (identification uncertain) (1022–94) and Minamoto Arihito (1103–47), respectively.
14. *The Somedono Minister . . . The Tale of Yotsugi*: Minister of State Fujiwara Yoshifusa (804–72). *The Tale of Yotsugi* (*Yotsugi no okina no monogatari*) is an alternative name for *Ōkagami* (*c.*1119), a historical tale centred on the glorious rule of Fujiwara

Michinaga (966–1027). The words quoted here are not found in any extant version.

15. *Prince Shōtoku*: Prince Umayado (574–622), revered early political figure and scholar, credited with having created Japan's first written constitution. This story appears in a collection of legends about his life (*Shōtoku taishi denreki*). It is generally interpreted to mean that he ordered the number of chambers in his tomb to be kept to a minimum as a way of ensuring his line would cease. The tomb was constructed several years before his death.

16. *the dews of Adashino's graves ... Toribe's burning grounds*: Adashino, north-west of the capital, and Toribe, to its south-east, were the two places where its dead were disposed of. They appear frequently in literature, along with the images of transient dew and a pyre's drifting smoke, as tropes for life's ephemerality.

17. *before forty at the latest*: It was commonly held that forty was the beginning of old age.

18. *a whiff of delightful incense ... a passing effect of robe-smoking*: Clothing was scented by being draped over a light frame to form a small tent within which incense was burned.

19. *The wizard priest of Kume*: A legendary figure, reputed to have been able to fly.

20. *how a woman's hair ... a woman's shoe*: There is a Buddhist legend about a net of human hair snaring an elephant. The reference to the flute made from a woman's shoe is untraceable.

21. *merely a transient habitation*: As in *Hōjōki*, this house is a Buddhist trope for the transience of physical existence.

22. *The Later Tokudaiji Minister*: Fujiwara Sanesada (1139–91). The word 'Later' was added to distinguish him from his father, also a minister.

23. *the poet-monk Saigyō*: (1118–90), a renowned poet. Saigyō had been employed by the Tokudaiji household before taking the tonsure at the age of twenty-three.

24. *Prince Ayanokōji*: Probably refers to the twelfth son of Emperor Kameyama (dates unknown).

25. *Kurusuno*: In the Yamashina area of present-day Kyoto.

26. *There is some pleasure ... quite forlorn*: This passage is somewhat confused, and there are differing interpretations of it.

27. *book spread before you*: The 'book' would probably be in the form of a scroll.

28. *Wenxuan ... Zhuangzi*: Famous Chinese classics. *Wenxuan* (Japanese *Monzen*), a compendious collection of prose and poetry down the ages; *Wenji* (Japanese *Monju*), a collection of the poems

of the popular Chinese poet Bai Juyi (Japanese Hakurakuten); the *Daode jing*, ancient Daoist text traditionally attributed to Laozi; *Zhuangzi,* a work assumed to be written by a man of that name, now attributed to Zhuang Zhou (?369–?286 BC).

29. *Japanese poetry*: *Waka*, poetry written in the Japanese language and following the 5-7-5-7-7 syllable construction, as distinct from poetry composed in Chinese and following the rules of Chinese prosody.

30. *The doings of lowly folk . . . lays his head*: The 'lowly folk' and 'mountain woodsmen' are stock images in *waka*.

31. *Ki no Tsurayuki's . . . the Kokinshū*: Ki no Tsurayuki (?872–?945) was one of the compilers and representative poets of the first great imperial poetry collection *Kokin wakashū* (or *Kokinshū*, *c.* 918). The poem is: 'No twining thread / my heart yet thins in parting / and as I travel on / away from you / it grows the more forlorn.'

32. *The Tale of Genji*: (*c.*1004–?12), famous early work of Japanese fiction by the court gentlewoman Murasaki Shikibu (?973–?1014). This variant on Ki no Tsurayuki's poem, in which *to ha nashi ni* replaces *to ha naku ni*, is quoted in Chapter 47, 'Agemaki'.

33. *Shinkokinshū . . . lonely on its peak*: Poem by Hafuribe no Narimochi (1180–?) in the second great imperial poetry collection, *Shinkokin wakashū* (or *Shinkokinshū*, 1205). The poem is: 'Winter comes / and the leaves fall / leaving the mountain bare. / Even the sole pine / is lonely on its peak.'

34. *Ienaga*: Minamoto Ienaga (?1170–1234), one of the compilers of the *Shinkokin wakashū*, who left a record of the experience in his diary.

35. *His Majesty*: Gotoba, who commissioned the *Shinkokin wakashū* and took an active part in its compilation.

36. *Ryōjin hishō*: A collection of popular songs (*c.* 1179) compiled by Goshirakawa.

37. *Kagura*: Literally 'god music'. This courtly shrine music was played ceremonially in the garden of the palace in the twelfth month.

38. *the flute . . . the six-stringed koto*: The flute referred to here may be the six-holed flute used in *kagura*. The *hichiriki* is a small, shrill reed flute, also used in *kagura*. The *biwa* is an instrument of the lute family, with four or five strings, played by plucking with a wide plectrum. The multi-stringed *koto* rests on the ground before the player.

39. *Xu You*: A legendary figure renowned for his purity and wisdom. This tale appears in *Meng qin*, as does the story of Sun Chen below.

40. *a 'singing gourd'*: (*Narihisako*), an alternative name for a gourd.
41. *'it is above all autumn . . . to tears'*: From an anonymous poem in the imperial poetry collection *Shūi wakashū* (*c.*1006). The poetic debate over which season, spring or autumn, is the more moving was of long standing. Autumn frequently won.
42. *The scented flowering orange . . . plum blossom . . . cherished memory*: These two flowers are strongly associated with memory in poetic tradition.
43. *the time of the Buddha's birthday . . . the Kamo festival*: There were special ceremonies surrounding the presumed date of the Buddha's birthday, on the eighth day of the fourth month. The Kamo festival, in the middle of the fourth month, was the most important festive occasion of the year. The fourth month in the old calendar marked the beginning of summer.
44. *sweet flag iris leaves are laid on roofs*: A custom performed on the fifth day of the fifth month, as a spell to protect the house from harm.
45. *the smoke . . . purifications of the sixth month*: Fires of dried grass, rice bran, etc. were lit to drive away mosquitoes. On the first day of the sixth month, ceremonies were performed at the water's edge to dispel evil spirits.
46. *The festival of Tanabata*: Originally from China, this festival held on the seventh day of the seventh month celebrated the yearly meeting in the heavens of the celestial lovers, the Weaver Star (Vega) and the Herdsman Star (Altair), who cross a bridge to briefly meet on this night.
47. *the garden stream*: This scene implies the garden of an aristocrat's house in the 'palace' style (*shinden-zukuri*), which traditionally had a stream constructed to run through it.
48. *people consider it too dreary to look at*: The waning moon of the twelfth month was traditionally considered particularly unattractive.
49. *The Litany of Buddha Names and the Presentation of Tributes*: The Litany of Buddha Names was an important service held at court at the end of the twelfth month, in which the names of the buddhas of the three worlds were chanted during a three-day period to pray for the extinction of sins. The Presentation of Tributes was performed by official tribute-bearers, who brought symbolic harvest offerings from the various provinces at New Year.
50. *the Worship of the Four Directions . . . the Great Demon Expulsion*: On the last night of the old year, demons believed to be the cause of plague and other calamities were ritually driven from

the palace. Before dawn the morning after the Great Demon Expulsion, the emperor performed an elaborate ritual worship of the four directions to ensure prosperity and protection from calamity in the coming year.

51. *the thick darkness of New Year's Eve*: New Year's Eve occurred on the last night of the lunar cycle, the night when the moon is dark.

52. *the ritual for dead souls*: Dead souls were believed to return in the seventh month, but formerly this was also believed to occur on New Year's Eve. Kenkō seems to have travelled to Kamakura and the eastern provinces on several occasions.

53. *new year pines*: In a tradition still observed today, pine branches were placed at the door of every home as a New Year decoration, perhaps originally as conduits to draw down the gods.

54. '*Day and night, the Yuan and Xiang . . . a grieving man*': A poem by the Chinese poet Dai Shulun (732–89).

55. *roving among mountain and stream . . . fish and birds*: A paraphrase of a poem by Xi Kang (223–62), found in *Wenxuan* (see note 28 above).

56. "*lift the carriage*" . . . "*raise up the flame*": The shift is in the form of the verbs, from *motage* and *kakage* to *moteage* and *kakiage*. The shafts of an ox carriage were raised in order to harness the ox. The flame is that of a lamp.

57. "*groundsmen to the standing lights*" . . . "*The Imperial Lecture Room*": The groundsmen (*tonomo*) saw to such matters as cleaning, lighting and heating in the palace. They are here being ordered to light the standing pine torches. In the middle of the fifth month, a five-day sutra reading and lecture was held in the emperor's presence in one of the palace rooms, which took its name from this ceremony.

58. *For all that the falling off . . . Ninefold Palace*: See note 21 to *Hōjōki* for 'latter days'. Ninefold Palace was an elegant term for the imperial palace.

59. *Places such as the Dew Platform . . . kojitomi, koitajiki or takayarido*: The Dew Platform (*rodai*) was an unroofed area linking the Shishinden and Jijūden buildings in the Inner Palace precinct. The Imperial Breakfast Room (*asagarei*) was the room in the emperor's residence where his breakfast was served. *Kojitomi* is a small window covered by a wooden-backed lattice shutter (*shitomi*). Although this and the following two items were common in houses, Kenkō finds the names redolent of the palace, where the words refer to specific places in certain buildings. *Koitajiki* is

a small wooden-floored area. *Takayarido* is a tall style of sliding door. The Gallery (*jin*) was the area where the nobles were seated to view and take part in court ceremonies.

60. *The Tokudaiji Minister*: Fujiwara Kintaka (1253–1305), a member of the Tokudaiji line of the Fujiwara clan who was Minister of State (*Ōkiotodo*) from 1302 to 1304, while Kenkō was employed at the palace.

61. *Sacred Mirror Room*: (*Naishidokoro*), the special room in the imperial palace where the Sacred Mirror, one of the Three Sacred Treasures of the Imperial House (*shingi*), was kept. A gentlewoman rang the bell three times after the emperor had viewed it.

62. *The seclusion . . . a most refined and delightful thing*: When a young girl from the imperial family was to become the next high priestess of the imperial Ise or Kamo shrines, she was first purified by a period of strict seclusion in the remote west of the capital, at a shrine named Nonomiya (the Shrine in the Fields). Kenkō is probably recalling the seclusion he would have witnessed as a young man in 1306.

63. *'child within' and 'dyed paper'*: Buddhist associations were held to sully the sanctity of the Shinto shrine, so euphemisms were employed for Buddhist words. The term 'child within' (*nakago*) may have derived from the placement of Buddhist statues in the heart of temple buildings. Sutras were frequently written on decorative dyed paper.

64. *the sacred fences . . . tied to the boughs of the sakaki tree*: Shrine buildings typically were surrounded by a wooden fence (*tamagaki*) and situated in a sacred grove. The *sakaki* tree (*Cleyera japonica*) is sacred to the gods, and in shrines its boughs often bear sacred paper streamers (*nusa*).

65. *Ise, Kamo, Kasuga . . . Matsuo and Umenomiya*: The locations of the shrines listed are: Ise Shrine on the Ise peninsula; Kamo, Hirano, Kibune, Ōharano, Matsuo, Umenomiya Shrines in the vicinity of the capital; Kasuga and Miwa Shrines in the vicinity of Nara; Sumiyoshi and Yoshida Shrines in the vicinity of Osaka.

66. *deeps and shallows of Asuka River*: A reference to an anonymous poem in the imperial anthology *Kokin wakashū*: 'What is there in this world / that remains unchanging? / The deeps of today's / Asuka River / tomorrow shift to shallows.'

67. *the peach and the plum tree . . . past things*: The first phrase quotes from a Chinese poem by Sugawara Funtoki (899–981). The second loosely quotes from a Japanese poem by Dewa no Ben.

68. *Kyōgoku-dono and Hōjōji Temple*: Kyōgoku-dono was the residence of the great ruler Fujiwara Michinaga (966–1027). A series of fires later destroyed it. Michinaga established Hōjōji Temple nearby, and lived there after he took the tonsure. It was also later destroyed by fire.
69. *The Midōdono*: The title used to refer to the great Fujiwara Michinaga (992–1074) after he took the tonsure.
70. *the Kondō . . . Shōwa era*: The Kondō, or Golden Hall, was the central structure in the temple precincts, where the image of the Buddha was housed. The Shōwa era was 1312–27.
71. *the Muryōju Hall*: The Muryōju Hall housed nine statues of Amitābha (Amida nyorai).
72. *calligraphy by Grand Counsellor Kōzei and the doors with Kaneyuki's writing*: Fujiwara Kōzei, or Yukinari (972–1027), was famed for his calligraphy, as was Minamoto Kaneyuki (dates unknown).
73. *Hokke-dō*: A hall devoted to the practice of meditation centred on *The Lotus Sutra* (*Hokke-kyō*).
74. *Thus did Mozi . . . the path's parting ways*: These two anecdotes are contained in the *Huainanzi* (attributed to Liu An, ?179–122 BC).
75. *Retired Emperor Horikawa's collection of one hundred poems*: *Horikawa-in ontoki hyakushu waka* (1099–1103), in which sixteen poets of the day composed 100 verses each, on set themes. This poem is by Fujiwara no Kinzane (1053–1107).
76. *the emperor's abdication ceremony*: It was usual at this time for the reigning emperor to abdicate early in favour of a successor. In 1318, when Kenkō was thirty-six, Emperor Hanazono abdicated in favour of his cousin Godaigo. The ceremony involved formally relinquishing the three sacred imperial insignia.
77. *The palace groundsmen . . . carpet the earth*: Composed by Hanazono.
78. *the emperor's year of mourning for a parent*: When the parent of an emperor died, he went into mourning for one year. He spent the first thirteen days confined in a specially built mourning 'hut', whose floor was lower than that of the palace buildings. Others also wore prescribed mourning clothes in sombre colours.
79. *How trying . . . services for the dead*: Reincarnation was believed to take forty-nine days, during which time frequent Buddhist services for the soul were held. Relatives of the deceased retired to

a place outside the city, such as a mountain temple, during this period.

80. *things that should be ritually avoided for the sake of the family*: There was a plethora of taboos involving ritual avoidance and abstinence (*imi*) after a death.
81. *'the dead grow more distant with each day'*: A line from an anonymous poem in the *Wenxuan* collection.
82. *When the present palace was constructed*: The palace of Emperor Hanazono, constructed in 1317.
83. *Genkimon-in*: (1246–1329), the mother of Emperor Fushimi. She would have been seventy-one at the time of this episode.
84. *the semi-circular 'comb' window in the Kan'in-dono*: A semi-circular hole cut into one of the walls at a specified place in the imperial palace. The name derives from the curved shape of the traditional Japanese boxwood comb. The Kan'in-dono was one of the emperor's alternative residences.
85. *'kaikō'*: Literally 'shell incense'. The operculum of the spindle whelk was ground to a powder and used in the production of incense.
86. *I saw some in the bay of Kanesawa in Musashino*: This memory dated from one of Kenkō's visits to Kamakura. Kanesawa is in present-day Yokohama.
87. *Hōnen*: Genkū (1133–1212), founder of the Jōdo sect, which taught that repeated chanting of the *nenbutsu* will ensure rebirth in paradise.
88. *Inaba*: Present-day Tottori prefecture.
89. *the horse racing at the Kamo Shrine*: Ceremonial horse racing took place at the Upper Kamo Shrine in the north of the capital to mark the fifth day of the fifth month.
90. *the Karahashi Captain*: Minamoto Masakiyo (1182–1230). He belonged to the Karahashi branch of the Minamoto family. There is no historical record of his son.
91. *those grotesque masks they wear in the Ni no Mai dance*: Ni no Mai was a comic interlude in the traditional court music and dance performance (*bugaku*: see also note 387 below), performed by two dancers wearing grotesque masks, one a laughing old man and the other a swollen-faced old woman.
92. *From a rough-woven bamboo door . . . deep violet gathered trousers*: The clothing suggests someone of high birth, and the scene hints at an aristocratic villa on the outskirts of the capital.
93. *Ox carriages stand about, propped on their empty shafts*: Guests and priests would have arrived in ox-drawn carriages, which

were left in the courtyard in the care of servants, with oxen unhitched and the shafts propped on boxes.

94. *'rough autumn fields'*: From a poem in the *Kokin Wakashū* by Henjō (816–90) which describes a garden so derelict it has returned to nature.

95. *Kinyo no Nii . . . Abbot Ryōgaku*: Fujiwara no Kinyo (?–1301) was known for his poetry. His brother Ryōgaku (dates unknown) was also a fine poet.

96. *Kiyomizu Temple*: An ancient temple in the eastern hills near the capital. An important place of pilgrimage down the centuries.

97. *kusame*: A word spoken as a protective spell when someone sneezed.

98. *I used to be wet nurse . . . Mount Hiei*: The old woman had been wet nurse to a son of an aristocratic family. The child had been made an acolyte of one of the prominent priests of the great temple of Enryakuji on Mount Hiei to the north-east of the capital, where he would be raised to attain priestly office.

99. *Count Mitsuchika*: Fujiwara Mitsuchika (1176–1221), a high-ranking and cultured courtier and a favourite of Emperor Gotoba.

100. *Sutra Lectures*: (*Saishō-kō*), lectures delivered at the palace over five days in the fifth month, to ritualistically ensure the peace of the nation.

101. *Having finished, he simply pushed . . . and left*: The room was partitioned by fine reed blinds from the adjoining area where the gentlewomen sat. It was the custom for a guest to remove his own standing tray (a tray with short legs on which food was served) if a servant was not present to do so. The precedent that so delighted the emperor is unclear.

102. *the corruptions of the world*: Attachment and delusion.

103. *The Ten Causes, Zenrin*: Zenrin was an alternative name for Yōkan (1032–1111), the seventh abbot of Zenrinji Temple in Kyoto. The central thesis of his treatise, whose full title is *The Ten Causes of Rebirth in Paradise*, was that chanting the *nenbutsu* (see *Hōjōki*, note 45) guaranteed instant rebirth in paradise.

104. *Shinkai*: A wandering recluse monk (dates unknown).

105. *the Ōchō period*: The reign of Emperor Hanazono.

106. *Ise . . . the capital and nearby Shirakawa*: The province of Ise (present-day Mie prefecture). Shirakawa, an area east of the Kamo River in present-day north-east Kyoto, was an outlying village at that time.

107. *Higashiyama to the Agui area*: He was crossing the capital to the north-west, having set out from the north-eastern edge around Shirakawa. The crowd was heading for the north-east edge of the city, near the Imade River. Ichijō Muromachi (the location of the platform from which the emperor viewed the Kamo festival) was in this vicinity.
108. *Kameyama Residence*: Retired Emperor Gosaga built the Kameyama Residence by the Ōi River to the west of the capital in 1255, on the site of present-day Tenryūji Temple.
109. *Uji*: An area to the south of the capital. Its fast-flowing river resulted in advanced water-wheel engineering skills among the locals.
110. *Ninnaji Temple . . . Iwashimizu Shrine*: Ninnaji Temple stood at the time on the northern edge of the capital. Iwashimizu Hachiman Shrine was an important pilgrimage site on the small Otoko Mountain, at the confluence of the Uji and Kizu Rivers south of the capital.
111. *Gokurakuji Temple and Kōra Shrine*: Two subsidiary sites of worship at the foot of Otoko Mountain. Pilgrims climbed the mountain to reach Iwashimizu Hachiman Shrine itself.
112. *a three-legged pot*: A decorative metal pot on three long legs.
113. *There was a beautiful young acolyte in Omuro*: The young boys who served in temples as acolytes were frequently the focus of adoring attention by older monks and priests. The name 'Omuro' strictly referred to the residence of the tonsured prince who was the abbot of Ninnaji, but more generally was synonymous with the temple itself.
114. *performing monks*: Monks who specialized in the arts of singing, dancing, etc.
115. *Narabigaoka Hill*: A wooded hill to the immediate south of Ninnaji.
116. *"kindle the autumn leaves to warm our wine"*: A well-known quotation from a poem by Bai Juyi: 'In the woods I kindle autumn leaves to warm my wine, / I brush the mossy stone to read a poem.' The monk playfully suggests that this would be the height of elegance.
117. *prove those magical powers . . . some miracle*: These monks belong to the esoteric Shingon sect, whose practice involves the chanting of mantras (phrases believed to carry magical powers) and performance of *mudras* (elaborate hand gestures with magical powers). Esoteric Buddhist priests were frequently called on to perform healing and other miracles.

118. *sliding door . . . wooden shutters*: Sliding doors can be pushed back to let in more light than the heavy wood-backed lattice shutters that swing open vertically, blocking light from above.
119. *the circumstances of some poem*: There was a long tradition of interest in anecdotes about the situation in which a poem might have been composed.
120. *The testament to our birth . . . escape from this world*: Rebirth in the human realm offers the chance to dedicate oneself to the Buddhist Way and thus transcend the cycle of rebirth.
121. *At Shinjōin Temple there once lived . . . Jōshin*: Shinjōin is a sub-temple in the Ninnaji Temple complex. Jōshin's dates are unknown.
122. *two hundred kan*: A substantial sum. A *kan* consisted of one hundred *hiki* (metal coins strung together through a hole in their centre).
123. *'Shiroururi'*: 'Shiro' probably means white, but the name is nonsensical.
124. *mass sutra readings*: Priests were commonly called upon to say sutras, often en masse, at the palace and aristocratic houses.
125. *the prescribed times*: Monks were formally permitted one meal a day, in the morning, although other meals at certain times were unofficially allowed.
126. *dropping a rice steamer from the roof when an imperial child is born*: An earthenware steamer was dropped from the roof, in the belief that this would encourage easy passage of the afterbirth.
127. *Ōhara*: A village to the north of the capital. 'Ōhara' is homophonous with a word meaning 'big belly'.
128. *Enseimon-in*: Esshi (1259–1332), daughter of Emperor Gosaga.
129. *With . . . yearn for you*: The little girl's poem is a simple riddle that describes the four phonetic characters *ko-i-shi-ku*, meaning lovingly.
130. *the Goshichinichi service*: A week-long Buddhist service held at the palace from the eighth day of the first month, to ensure prosperity and peace for the coming year. It was traditionally led by the holiest priest of Tōji Temple.
131. *an ox carriage with five-corded screens*: Types of carriage were strictly regulated according to social standing. The ox-drawn carriage was reserved for people of high rank. The reed screens hung at front, back and sides could be decorated with coloured cords, the use and number of which was dependent on rank.
132. *formal lacquered cap*: (*Kanmuri, kōburi*), a flat cap with raised section at the back and stiff gauze tail or other attachments, worn for formal events at court.

133. *The Okamoto Chancellor*: Fujiwara Iehira (1282–1324).

134. *two opposing diagonal cuts, the second being roughly half an inch deep*: I.e. cut not with a single stroke, but by first cutting diagonally a certain way through one side, then making a second diagonal cut from the other side.

135. *walking in the prescribed manner*: Certain dance-like movements seem to have been prescribed for the occasion.

136. *wing building*: Possibly refers to a section of the house leading off from the north-east of the main building, used for meeting with people come on business and other informal purposes.

137. *gift of clothing . . . gestures of thanks*: People who delivered messages or other things were usually rewarded by the gift of one or several robes. There was a prescribed series of ritual gestures to be made in thanks for a gift.

138. *'These flowers I pluck for you, my lord / know nothing of time'*: Two lines from a poem in section 98 of *The Tales of Ise* (*Ise monogatari*, late ninth or early tenth century). The words 'know nothing of time' (*toki shi mo wakanu*) contain a pun on the word for 'pheasant' (*ki shi = kiji*).

139. *the Iwamoto and Hashimoto subshrines within the Kamo Shrine*: These two tiny shrines still stand in the grounds of Kamigamo Shrine, in northern Kyoto, one (Iwamoto) on a prominent rock, the other (Hashimoto) near the bridge over the shrine stream.

140. *Narihira and Sanekata*: Ariwara no Narihira (825–80) was a great poet whose supposed amorous exploits are described together with many of his poems in *The Tales of Ise*. The courtier and poet Fujiwara no Sanekata (d. 998) died during a remote posting which he received as punishment for a quarrel. There was a legend that his ghost haunted the Kamo Shrine stream.

141. *Abbot Yoshimizu's poem*: Yoshimizu (1155–1225) was a renowned poet usually known by his ecclesiastical name Jien. This poem plays on the *ari* of the name Ariwara, which means 'to be or exist'.

142. *Lady Konoe*: Dates unknown. She was gentlewoman to Empress Kishi (1252–1318). Her poems were included in six imperial poetry collections.

143. *Tsukushi*: The island of Kyushu.

144. *The holy man of Shosha*: Seikū (?909–1007), who founded a temple on Mount Shosha in Harima (modern Hyōgo prefecture).

145. *The Lotus Sutra . . . the Six Senses*: *The Lotus Sutra* (*Saddharma pundarīka-sūtra*) is a key text of Mahayana Buddhism. Eyes, ears,

nose, tongue, body and mind are held to lead humans to stray from the Buddhist Way.

146. *During the Gen'ō era . . . the Seishodō*: Gen'ō was the era name for the years of Emperor Godaigo's reign (1318–39). Treasured instruments were given names, such as Genshō and Bokuba. 'Genshō' had been stolen in 1316. This concert, held in the musical performance hall at the palace (Seishodō), was part of the elaborate musical performances that followed the new emperor's accession ceremonies in 1318.
147. *the Kikutei Minister*: Fujiwara no Kanesue (1283–1339).
148. *a private worship hall*: The pious well-to-do built a hall in the grounds of their home for private worship. The altar could become cluttered with a variety of Buddhist images.
149. *a supplicatory prayer*: *Ganmon*, a written document presented at the altar, praying for specified outcomes and listing the virtues of the supplicant. These could include the construction of temples or Buddhist images, copying of sutras and giving of alms.
150. *The Great Cessation and Insight*: (*Maka shikan*), an important manual of Tendai meditation practice by Chih-i (538–97), as recorded by a disciple.
151. *fine silk covers*: Fine silk was used to cover bound books (*sōshi*), and as the covering wrap of a scroll (*makimono*). A scroll's cylindrical roller was sometimes elegantly lacquered and inlaid with mother-of-pearl, etc.
152. *Ton'a*: (1289–1372), priest of the Pure Land sect. Ton'a was a well-known poet and scholar contemporaneous with Kenkō.
153. *Bishop Kōyū*: Dates unknown. A priest at Ninnaji and probable friend of Kenkō.
154. *Chikurin'in Novice and Minister of the Left*: Saionji Kinhira (1264–1315). He became Minister of the Left in 1309, and took the tonsure in 1311.
155. *Tōin Minister of the Left*: Fujiwara Saneyasu (1269–1327). He became Minister of the Left in 1318.
156. *Fa Xian*: (337–*c.* 422, Japanese Hokken). He travelled to India in 399, and carried back and translated a number of Buddhist sutras.
157. *the saintly Emperor Shun*: A legendary Chinese emperor renowned for his perfection. This passage consists of loose quotations from Confucian texts.
158. *Counsellor Koretsugu*: Taira Koretsugu (1266–1343).
159. *Miidera Temple . . . the Bunpō era*: Miidera (an alternative name for Onjōji), was an important temple complex of the Tendai sect

at the foot of Mount Hiei, rival of the great Enryakuji on Mount Hiei. In 1319 warrior monks from Enryakuji stormed and burned Miidera. En'i (dates unknown) was known for his poetic talent. Koretsugu was probably studying under him at the time of this story. The Bunpō era was 1317–19.

160. *a very clever thing to say*: The term 'Temple Monk' distinguished the monks of Miidera from those of Mount Hiei, who were referred to as 'Mountain Monks'.

161. *Gukaku*: Nothing is known of Gukaku. He was probably a lay monk, still living at home.

162. *when they reached Kohata . . . Nara monks*: Kohata is en route from Kyoto to Uji. Warrior monks from the big temples in the old capital of Nara were renowned for their ferocity.

163. *Wakan rōeishū*: 'Japanese and Chinese Poems to Sing'. A collection of Chinese and Japanese poems compiled early in the eleventh century by Fujiwara Kintō (966–1041), referred to here as the Shijō Grand Counsellor.

164. *Ono no Tōfū*: (896–966), died the year Fujiwara Kintō was born.

165. *a certain Amidabutsu . . . linked verse*: 'Amidabutsu' (Amitābha Buddha) was appended to the name of the monks of sects such as the Ji, whose worship focused on Amitābha. The name was commonly associated with specialists in linked verse (*renga*), a communal verse-making activity.

166. *The Dainagon Abbot . . . Otozuru-maru . . . Yasura-dono*: None of these is identifiable. It was common practice for young acolytes to receive the sexual attentions of older men.

167. *I've never seen his head*: If he were a full monk, his head would be shaved.

168. *Yin-Yang masters*: (*Onmyōji*), professional practitioners of Yin-Yang divination (*onmyōdō*), a complex divinatory system inherited from China.

169. *'Red Tongue Days'*: Named for the red-tongued demon whose turn it is to guard the western gate of Jupiter every six days, in the elaborate mythology underlying the traditional almanac inherited from China. Auspicious and inauspicious days, calculated with complex methods by the Yin-Yang masters, played an important part in life.

170. *two arrows in his hand*: It was the practice to take up two arrows at a time when shooting.

171. *The Tokiwai Chief Minister*: Saionji Sanemune (1194–1269).

172. *the ring for the cord . . . lacquered box*: Lidded lacquered boxes, often elaborately decorated with inlay designs, were a common

household item, used for holding documents or sundry personal effects such as combs. They were tied with a cord, which was passed through a decorative ring set into a small hollow on one side below the lid edge.

173. *the "roller" or left side . . . the "cover" or right*: The conventional names for the left and right sides of the box apparently derived from analogy to a hand scroll, which unrolls with the cylindrical roller on the left, and the scroll's cover page on the right.
174. *a plant called menamomi*: This plant has not been satisfactorily identified. It may be a form of wild tobacco.
175. *An honourable man has moral imperatives*: This echoes ideas found in Taoist teachings, which describe the strict pursuit of Confucian-style morality as a deviation from one's essential nature.
176. *Superb Small Sermons*: (*Ichigon hōdan*), an anonymous collection of the short teachings of thirty-four revered Buddhist teachers, probably dating from the early fourteenth century.
177. *a pickling jar*: A ceramic jar for storing vegetables preserved in rice bran and salt.
178. *a fine copy of the sutras or a nicely made Buddhist image*: The Buddhist sutras and an image for private worship were the two most important possessions for a serious Buddhhist aspirant.
179. *The Horikawa Chief Minister*: Koga no Mototomo (1232–97).
180. *Lord Mototoshi*: Koga no Mototoshi (1261–1319). Mototomo's second son, and younger brother of Tomomori, whom Kenkō served as a young man. He was Director of Police from 1285 to 1286.
181. *The Koga Chief Minister . . . Privy Chamber*: The Koga Chief Minister was Minamoto no Michimitsu (1187–1248). The Privy Chamber was the room at the palace where senior courtiers and court nobles gathered when on duty.
182. *Bring a wooden vessel*: This appears to be an instance of correcting behaviour in accordance with court precedent. 'Wooden vessel' is the generally agreed interpretation of the mysterious *magari* that he asks for.
183. *Conveyor of Documents Yasutsuna*: Nakahara Yasutsuna (1290–1339). It was his duty to deliver the documents created by the Compiler of Documents.
184. *Grand Counsellor Count Mitsutada*: Koga Mitsutada (1284–1331). It is unclear when he took the tonsure.
185. *Tōin Minister of the Right*: Not identified.
186. *Matagorō*: Not identified.
187. *the Konoe Minister*: Fujiwara Tsunetada (1302–52).

188. *the Daikakuji Palace*: The residence of Retired Emperor Gouda from 1308 until his death.
189. *the physician Tadamori*: Tanba Tadamori (?–1344).
190. *Lord Kin'akira*: Sanjō Kin'akira (1282–1336). He became Acting Grand Counsellor the year he died.
191. *a Chinese sake flask*: The elaborate joke is in reference to the famous warrior from Ise, Taira Tadamori, whose squint occasioned the joke 'the Ise sake flask [*heiji*, homophonous with an alternative reading of "Taira family"] is a vinegar flask [*sugame*, homophonous with the word for "squint"]'. Tanba Tadamori's forebears were Chinese.
192. *worship hall*: (*Midō*), a small building in the compound of a house, housing a Buddhist image and devoted to worship.
193. *Shōkū . . . the great monastery on Mount Kōya*: Shōkū is unidentified. The monastic complex on Mount Kōya, several days' ride from the capital in present-day Wakayama prefecture, is the centre of the Shingon sect.
194. *In the days of Retired Emperor Kameyama*: Kameyama held this position from 1274 until his death.
195. *whether he had heard the hototogisu sing yet*: The *hototogisu*, a kind of cuckoo, calls for a brief period in early summer. The song is celebrated in poetry, so the question is a test of the man's poetic sensibility.
196. *'A man of no account . . . the ears to hear it'*: This reply makes elegant reference to several poems from the anthologies.
197. *'I believe I heard one at Iwakura,' . . . the Horikawa Palace Minister's*: The minister was Minamoto no Tomomori (1249–1316). Iwakura, a village to the north of the capital, was famous for its *hototogisu* in spring. Tomomori had a country villa there.
198. *the Jōdoji Chancellor*: Probably refers to Fujiwara Moronori (1273–1320).
199. *Ankimon'in*: (1207–86), Moronori's great-aunt.
200. *The Yamashina Minister of the Left*: Fujiwara Saneo (1217–73).
201. *What entertainment could you find*: The translation here follows the Shōtetsu-bon text.
202. *Xie Lingyun*: (385–433), important landscape poet, who was executed on suspicion of plotting rebellion. No record exists of his part in the translation of *The Lotus Sutra* into Chinese.
203. *Hui Yuan . . . Bailian group*: Hui Yuan (334–416) established the temple of Donglinsi on Mount Lu. His Bailian (Japanese Byakuren, White Lotus) group was dedicated to achieving rebirth in paradise through chanting of Amida's name.

204. *kickball*: *Mari* or *kemari*, a courtly game in which players attempted to keep a soft leather ball in the air as long as possible by kicking it to each other.
205. *sugoroku*: A board game whose primary aim was to remove all your pieces (known as 'horses') from the board as quickly as possible with throws of the dice.
206. *go*: A popular board game played with numerous small counters or 'stones' by two people seated at a low table.
207. *the Four Transgressions or the Five Wickednesses*: Buddhist teaching places in the Four Transgressions the serious sins of killing, theft, adultery and lying. The Five Wickednesses are: murdering one's mother, father or a Buddhist adept, causing discord among harmonious groups of monks, and causing blood to flow from a buddha's body.
208. *'Night closes in . . . on life's road'*: Lines lamenting the approach of death after an unfulfilled life, attributed to the Chinese poet Bai Juyi.
209. *the Imadegawa Minister*: Saionji Kinsuke (1223–67).
210. *Tamenori*: Unidentified.
211. *the Uzumasa Lord*: Unidentified, but possibly Fujiwara Nobukiyo (1159–1216).
212. *were given interesting names*: The names all seem to relate to oxen, but their meanings are unclear. The names differ in variant texts.
213. *boro priests*: As this anecdote reveals, *boro* were rough, itinerant men who displayed all the markings of Buddhist renunciates, but combined their austerities with a fondness for the sword that made them more like outlaws.
214. *Shukugahara*: Probably the place of that name in present-day Kanagawa prefecture.
215. *the Nine Nenbutsus*: Chants associated with rebirth into the nine levels of the Pure Land paradise.
216. *boronji, bonji or kanji*: This proliferation of alternative names suggests that the *boro* were not a formal religious group but a haphazard community of itinerant Buddhist practitioners that existed on the edges of society.
217. *the water-heating room*: A small room near the kitchen in the palace and other noble residences, where water was heated and eating utensils kept.
218. *the black lacquered cupboard . . . the Kitayama Novice*: The cupboard was presumably one found in the water-heating room, although the term generally referred to an item of furniture used

for such things as ladies' combs and other personal items. The Kitayama Novice (Saionji Sanekane: see also note 428) (1249–1322), was the father of Empress Kishi (?–1333), who was the consort of Emperor Godaigo.

219. *the classics speak of . . . hard to come by*: The first quotation is from the ancient classic *Shu jing* (*The Book of Documents*), the second is from *Laozi* (third century BC, anonymous).

220. *the stony heart of a Jie or a Zhou*: Jie (1728–1675 BC) and Zhou (r. 1075–1046 BC) were both kings renowned for their cruelty and immorality.

221. *Wang Huizhi*: (321–79) a noted Chinese littérateur and calligrapher. There is no known record of his love of birds.

222. *the classic*: These words are found in *Shu jing*.

223. *an aid to learning*: Laborious copying of texts was an important part of study at the time.

224. *the Six Arts*: Manners, music, archery, equestrianship, calligraphy and arithmetic.

225. *The monk Zehō . . . the Pure Land sect*: Zehō (dates unknown) was a poet and recluse monk contemporaneous with Kenkō. The Pure Land (Jōdo) sect, a Buddhist sect immensely popular at the time, taught that rebirth in the Pure Land of Amitābha could be achieved through conscientious chanting of his name.

226. *the forty-ninth-day ceremony after a death*: The forty-ninth day marks the end of the initial rites of prayer for a soul after death.

227. *a Chinese dog*: The man was attempting to praise the priest by comparing him to this precious foreign dog.

228. *gambling*: Gambling was common with the board games of *go* and *sugoroku*, but here it probably refers to simple dice-throwing.

229. *Grand Counsellor Masafusa*: Tsuchimikado Masafusa (1262–1302).

230. *Yan Hui's . . . avoid burdening others*: Yan Hui (521–490 BC) was a great sage, and the primary disciple of Confucius. The reference is to *Analects* V, 25. Kenkō's interpretation relies on an alternative understanding of the sentence, not generally accepted today.

231. *One should not . . . the humble man*: This sentence is somewhat garbled. One interpretation is offered here. As in the previous sentence, Kenkō's interpretation of the *Analects* (IX, 25) is at odds with the accepted meaning.

232. *The joys . . . reality of this life*: According to Buddhist teaching, the phenomenal world is fundamentally illusory.

233. *think of the man . . . fear at the height*: A reference to a story originally from China but repeated in Japanese texts.

234. *The name of the Toba Road . . . after the Toba Palace was built*: The Toba Road led to the Toba Palace, which was built in 1086 by Emperor Shirakawa (1053–1129) to the south of the capital.

235. *The Rihō Prince's Diary*: The diary of Prince Shigeaki (906–54), son of Emperor Daigo. Rihō is the Sinified name of the Ministry of Ceremonial (Shikibu-shō), of which Shigeaki was the titular head.

236. *Prince Motoyoshi's recitation . . . Daikokuden*: The ceremony held at the Daikokuden building in the imperial palace on the morning of New Year's Day included a recitation, by a high-ranking person, of the First Day Felicitations to the emperor. Motoyoshi (890–943) was the eldest son of Emperor Yōzei.

237. *built in the shinden style*: A style of aristocratic architecture based around a central sleeping area (*shinden*), surrounded by an outer space that could be enclosed by shutters, beyond which was a veranda.

238. *the north should be avoided as inauspicious*: Perhaps because the dead are laid out facing north.

239. *the great shrine of Ise*: The most important, and possibly the most ancient, Shinto shrine in Japan, located in present-day Mie prefecture. It is dedicated to the Sun Goddess (Amaterasu-ōmikami), believed to be the ancestor of the imperial line.

240. *A certain samādhi monk . . . Retired Emperor Takakura's tomb*: A monk who performed meditation and sutra chanting. The Lotus Hall, dedicated to worship of the *Lotus Sutra*, stood at the site of Takakura's tomb.

241. *the Novice Grand Counsellor Sukesue . . . the Captain and Consultant Tomouji*: Fujiwara no Sukesue (1207–89) and Minamoto no Tomouji (1232–75). Sukesue was respected for his knowledge of court lore.

242. *muma no kitsuriyō . . . kuren tō*: An apparently meaningless jumble of sounds.

243. *the late retired emperor . . . imperial physician Atsushige*: The retired emperor was Gouda. Wake Atsushige (dates unknown) was in charge of the emperor's kitchens, a post that required a detailed knowledge of food.

244. *Herbal Compendium*: *Honzōgaku*, a scholarly work that described not only herbs and plants in general but also animals and minerals.

245. *former Palace Minister Rokujō*: Minamoto Arifusa (1251–1319).

246. *what is the left-side radical of the character for "salt"*: This is a trick question. The word was most correctly written with a complex character whose radical is at the bottom. However, it was commonly replaced by a simpler version, which Atsushige's answer describes.
247. *To long for the moon . . . passes unseen*: The first phrase echoes a common subject for Chinese poetry. The second is a reference to a poem by Fujiwara Yoruka (fl. *c*.875): 'As I lay in my curtained room / unknowing while the Spring / passed me by unseen / the blossoms I watched and waited for / had faded and gone.'
248. *indulging in linked verse-making together*: Group composition of linked poetry was a popular pastime among commoners at this time.
249. *the blinds*: The temporary viewing stands erected for the festival were hung with reed blinds through which those of more delicate sensibility could watch the procession while remaining hidden from view.
250. *that section of the procession*: The long procession to the shrine was broken into separate sections, with some time between each.
251. *strewn with the emblematic aoi leaves*: The heart-shaped leaf of the *aoi* (sometimes translated as 'hollyhock'), emblem of the Kamo (or Aoi) festival, was liberally used to decorate the route of the procession.
252. *It is this that is the real point of seeing the festival*: I here follow the Shōtetsu-bon and Jōen-bon texts. Other variants have: 'To see the streets is to see the festival.'
253. *Toribe, Funaoka*: The two big burning grounds for corpses in the capital, Toribe to the south-east and Funaoka to the north-west.
254. *mamakodate*: Literally 'choosing the stepchild'. Fifteen black and fifteen white pieces are put side by side in a circle or rectangle according to complicated rules. One piece at a time is removed by a series of counts, until only one is left.
255. *Suhō no Naishi*: Dates unknown. She served in the court of Retired Emperor Shirakawa, and was renowned for her poetic skills.
256. *How pointless now . . . cannot see them with me*: A poem sent to another gentlewoman with whom she had shared a room, but who had now left the court. The poem relies on a series of puns, such as *misu* (blind) and *mizu* (not seen).
257. *The Pillow Book . . . a dried sprig of aoi*: *The Pillow Book* (early eleventh century), a compendium of apparently random lists, anecdotes, opinions and musings by a gentlewoman at the emp-

ress's court, Sei Shōnagon (?966–?1025), which is one of the great classics of Japanese literature. These are the opening words of section 27.

258. *Tales of the Four Seasons*: (*Shiki monogatari*). It is now considered doubtful that Kamo no Chōmei was the author of this undated work.

259. *The herbal balls . . . ninth-month chrysanthemums*: For the festival of the fifth day of the fifth month, small bags containing herbs and iris stalks, and decorated with flowers and coloured threads, were hung around the curtained dais (a raised area, roofed and hung with curtains, in the inner chamber). The balls remained through the summer, and were replaced by chrysanthemums for the festival of the ninth day of the ninth month.

260. *Ben no Menoto . . . 'though yet the irises remain'*: On the death of the dowager empress (Fujiwara Kenshi, 994–1027), the imperial nurse Ben no Menoto (dates unknown) composed a poem containing these words, which weaves a complex double meaning of puns around the image of the dead irises. The responding poem of another gentlewoman, Gō Jijū (dates unknown), also depends on a complex play of words.

261. *The cherries of Yoshino and the Left Guard cherry*: Yoshino, a mountain south of Nara, was renowned even then for its cherry trees. The Left Guard cherry and the Right Guard *tachibana* (decorative mandarin) traditionally grew one on either side of the stairs of the Shishinden in the Inner Palace.

262. *The Kyōgoku Counsellor Novice*: The great poet and critic Fujiwara Teika (Sadaie) (1162–1241).

263. *tachibana and katsura*: The decorative mandarin (*Citrus tachibana*) and *katsura* (*Cercidiphyllum japonicum*) were common garden trees.

264. *Gyōren of Hiden-in*: Gyōren is unknown. Hiden-in, a temple that took in orphans and invalids, was in the north of Kyoto. His clan name of Miura reveals that he came from the eastern provinces.

265. *the holy man of Toganowo*: Myōe (1173–1232), founder of Kōsanji Temple on Toganowo Mountain, north of the capital.

266. *'Ashi! Ashi!'*: Literally 'Leg! Leg!' The saintly Myōe mishears this as *Aji*, the name of the first vowel in Sanskrit and, in the esoteric Buddhist tradition to which Myōe belonged, a powerful religious symbol of the origin of all things.

267. *the Fushō*: A low-ranking member of the Palace Guards. Myōe mistakes this name for its homonym, a word conveying the

Buddhist doctrine of the non-existence of birth and death, expressed in the term *aji hon fushō*. Understanding of the nature of *aji* brings about a realization of *fushō*.

268. *What virtue I have gained from this encounter*: It was believed that an encounter with a saintly person caused a transfer of virtue to the other.
269. *imperial bodyguard Hada no Shigemi*: (Dates unknown). The Hada family traditionally provided expedition guards (*zuiin*), guards who accompanied aristocrats and members of the imperial family when they left their residences.
270. *the Shimotsuke Novice Shingan*: No record of him exists.
271. *Abbot Meiun*: (1115–83), abbot of the great Enryakuji Temple. He was struck by a stray arrow.
272. *unfit to perform worship before the gods*: The ugly scars left from burning curative moxa on the skin constitute a kind of impurity, which would offend the gods.
273. *the Three Ri*: The name of the three moxibustion points on the outside of the leg below the kneecap.
274. *new deer antler*: A powder made from a deer's budding spring antlers was a popular tonic in traditional medicine.
275. *The holy priest Jōnen of Saidaiji Temple*: Ryōchō (1252–1331), head of the ancient temple of Saidaiji outside Nara.
276. *the Saionji Palace Minister*: Saionji Sanehira (1290–1326).
277. *Count Suketomo*: Hino Suketomo (1290–1332).
278. *When Grand Counsellor Novice Tamekane . . . the Rokuhara Commissary*: Kyōgoku no Tamekane (1254–1332), a leading poet of his day. He was arrested and exiled in 1298 as a result of his allegiance to the rival imperial faction. Later pardoned, he was rearrested in 1316, the incident referred to here. The Rokuhara Commissary was the local headquarters of the Kamakura government, which was in effective control of the nation.
279. *That's the ideal kind of memory . . . having lived*: Suketomo in fact achieved a similar end, being executed for his part in an uprising at the age of forty-three.
280. *Tōji Temple*: A large temple at the southern edge of the capital.
281. *The Uji Minister of the Left*: Fujiwara no Yorinaga (1120–56). Kenkō seems to have confused the details of this story.
282. *"fish road" . . . where your lips have been*: Apparently based on an elegant conceit whereby the sake, like fish which follow an accustomed path through the ocean, should be swilled back over the place it had passed before.

283. *mina-musubi*: A style of plaiting used in the making of decorative cords. *Mina* was the name for a type of edible snail.
284. *hanging a sign on the gate*: The name of a temple, palace building, etc. was usually written on a board attached to the front gate.
285. *The Kadenokōji Second-rank Novice*: Fujiwara Tsunemasa (1246–?), a renowned calligrapher.
286. *temporary awnings*: Cloth stretched over four uprights to provide shelter for viewers of outdoor events.
287. *a sacred goma fire*: From the Sanskrit *homa*. A rite performed by certain Buddhist sects in which small wooden sticks are burned as a form of magical invocation.
288. *The bishop of Seikanji . . . as gyōhō*: Dōga (1284–1343), poet and friend of Kenkō. Seikanji was a temple in the south-east of the capital. *Gyōhō* is a Buddhist term, referring to the ritual incantatory rites performed together with the *goma* ceremony. In compound words, an 'h' is commonly, but not always, hardened to 'b'.
289. *the first day of spring*: This was calculated by the angle of the sun, and usually occurred in early February.
290. *Henzōji Temple*: A Shingon temple in the north-west of the capital.
291. *Grand Counsellor Mototoshi*: See note 180 above.
292. *the 'tai' . . . the extra stroke*: Yin-Yang divination used special names for the months. The character *tai* (large) retained its pronunciation but became a character meaning 'dog' by the addition of a single stroke.
293. *Morichika . . . the Konoe Chancellor*: Fujiwara Morichika (dates unknown). He took the tonsure in 1336. The identity of the Konoe Chancellor is unclear.
294. *a divination report in the hand of Yoshihira himself*: Divination reports (*senmon* or *urakata*) were presented by a Yin-Yang master to the emperor at times of untoward events such as earthquakes or famine. Abe no Yoshihira (fl. early eleventh century) was renowned for his divination skills.
295. *a monk from either the esoteric or exoteric schools*: The esoteric sects (*mikkyō*), such as Tendai and Shingon, termed the others, such as Pure Land, 'exoteric' (*kenkyō*), since their teachings were clearly expressed and accessible to all rather than based on secret teachings.
296. *the term shiki . . . often combined with something else*: This term, meaning 'prescribed way of doing something', could be used either

alone or in such combinations as *hōshiki* (much the same meaning). It is claimed here that the latter was a recent development.

297. *Ukyō no Daibu . . . unchanged*: Kenreimon'in (1155–1213) was the consort of Emperor Takakura, but became embroiled in the famous sea battle of Dannoura in 1185, after which she retired to a nunnery. Ukyō no Daibu (dates unknown) served her at the palace, and later became a gentlewoman in the court of Gotoba after his accession in 1183. She was a skilled poet. The words quoted here are from her poetry collection *Kenreimon'in Ukyō no Daibu-shū*, and bewail the mournful changes she has witnessed since she last served there.

298. *Ruan Ji's 'welcoming green eyes'*: Chinese littérateur and philosopher (210–63), whose eyes were said to be white for unwanted guests and green for those he welcomed.

299. *a game of shell matching*: This popular game involved accumulating matching clam shells. The rules of the version described here are unknown.

300. *When you place a piece . . . as you flick it*: A game played with a *go* board, in which the aim is to knock pieces from your opponent's side.

301. *the closest black circle*: The *go* board is divided into 324 squares, which in turn consist of nine larger squares marked by small black circles at their corners. The exact nature of the game described here is unknown.

302. *the Chinese sage Duke Xiao of Qing*: The posthumous name of Zhao Pu (eleventh century), councillor to three generations of emperor. These words are found in his *Record of Meritorious Officials* (*Ming chen yan xing lu*).

303. *Book of Medicine:* Found in the preface to the ancient herbal compendium *Shen Nong Ben Cao Jing*.

304. *The legendary emperor Yu . . . setting off to defeat the Miao*: Recorded in *Shu jing* (*The Book of Documents*). The Miao were a group of rebellious tribes on the outskirts of the empire.

305. *'a long life lies ruined'*: From Bai Juyi's poem 'On Drawing a Silver Jar from the Well'.

306. *the poet Ono no Komachi . . . the saint of Mount Kōya, Kōbō Daishi*: Ono no Komachi's dates are indeed unknown. A great poet, she flourished from 833 until 857. *Tamatsukuri Komachi Sōsuisho*, an anonymous mid-Heian work, describes the beauty and eventual decline of the poet. No record exists of the courtier Miyoshi no Kiyoyuki (847–918) as its author. Kōbō Daishi is the affectionate name for Kūkai (774–835), founder of the Shingon

sect of Buddhism and its great monastery on Mount Kōya. Several works refer to him as the author of the *Sōsuisho*, but the attribution is clearly an error.

307. *It is said that a dog . . . if used with large hawks*: Smaller hawks such as falcons were used for the autumn sport of birding, while winter hunting of pheasants and rabbits used larger species such as the goshawk.

308. *'the greatest of medicines'*: A quotation from *Han shu* (AD 32–92), a famous history of the Han dynasty.

309. *the Buddha teaches . . . five hundred lifetimes without hands*: From a passage found in the *Bonmō Sutra* (fifth century?).

310. *the Black Door*: A small room in the emperor's palace.

311. *When the Komatsu emperor ascended the throne*: Emperor Kōkō, who took the throne at the late age of fifty-five after a life of relatively humble status.

312. *indulged in making his own meals there*: Although the sentence euphemistically suggests this was a game, his straitened circumstances prior to his accession make it probable that he cooked for himself from necessity.

313. *the Kamakura Central Affairs Bureau Prince*: Prince Munetaka (1243–74). This episode took place at his residence in Kamakura, where he was shōgun from 1252 to 1266.

314. *The Oki Governor Novice Sasaki*: Sasaki Masayoshi (1208–90). He was governor of Oki Province, and later took the tonsure.

315. *the Yoshisada Middle Captain*: His identity is unclear.

316. *kagura dancing . . . the Sacred Sword*: *Kagura* is a combination of music and dance performed as a sacred rite to celebrate the gods. On this occasion, it was performed in the room in the emperor's palace that held the Sacred Mirror. The dancer is described as performing with the Sacred Sword, another of the Three Sacred Treasures of the Imperial House.

317. *Imperial Day Chamber*: The room in the palace which the emperor occupied during the day.

318. *The holy priest Dōgen . . . singling out the Surangama Samadhi Sutra*: Dōgen (dates unknown). He went to China to further his Buddhist studies around 1309. (To be distinguished from the more famous Dōgen (1200–1253) who founded the Sōtō sect of Zen Buddhism.) The Complete Sutras (*issaikyō*) were copied as a pious act. Among them is the *Surangama Samadhi* (Japanese *Shuregon*) *Sutra*. Rokuhara was an area at the south-east edge of the capital. The original Nālandā (Japanese Naranda) Temple, in

central India, was founded at the beginning of the fifth century, and was an important centre of Buddhism.

319. *the Ōe Governor*: Ōe no Masafusa (1041–1111).

320. *the Xi yu and Fa Xian*: The *Xi yu* (*Da Tang xi yu ji*) is a detailed account of the travels of the monk Xuanzang (602–64) through India. The *Fa Xian* refers to the record Fa Xian (see note 156 above) wrote of his travels in India and Ceylon.

321. *Xi Ming Monastery*: A large temple founded by Xuanzang in the Chinese capital Chang'an. There was debate in Japan over its orientation because Daianji Temple in Nara was said to have been modelled on it but faced south.

322. *The ceremony known as Sagichō . . . the Shinsen Garden in the palace*: Sagichō was one of the names gives to a fire ceremony performed at the palace on the fifteenth and eighteenth days of the new year. Bat-and-ball games were traditionally played at New Year. The Shingon-in was a building in the imperial palace complex devoted to religious devotions. The Shinsen Garden was a large garden in the south of the palace complex where banquets and religious ceremonies were held.

323. *the cry 'The Law-fulfilling Pond!'*: The Shinsen Garden pond was the site of invocation ceremonies to pray for rain. This cry or song was apparently chanted as part of the ceremony described here.

324. *'Tamba' is apparently a mistake for tamare*: Tamba is a region in the mountains north-west of Kyoto.

325. *The tale . . . in The Diary of Sanuki no Suke*: A journal by the court gentlewoman Fujiwara no Nagako (*c.* 1079–?). The incident is recorded as happening in 1108.

326. *The Shijo Grand Counsellor Count Takachika*: Fujiwara Takachika (1203–79), a man renowned for his culinary knowledge.

327. *such vulgar stuff should not be served to His Majesty*: The objection apparently was to the salmon in its dried form. As Takachika points out, salmon itself was considered acceptable.

328. *The Matsushita nun*: Dates unknown. She took the tonsure on the death of her husband Hōjō Tokiuji in 1230.

329. *Tokiyori, Governor of Sagami*: Hōjō Tokiyori (1227–63) was the fifth regent of the Kamakura government. He became Governor of Sagami Province in 1249.

330. *Castle Deputy Yoshikage*: Adachi Yoshikage (1210–53), Deputy of Akita Castle, a nominal title.

331. *repairing each ripped square in turn*: The screen is divided into a series of small squares by wooden crosspieces. A sheet of thin paper is glued on to the frame of each square.

332. *Castle Deputy and Governor of Mutsu Yasumori*: Adachi Yasumori (1231–85). He inherited the title Deputy of Akita Castle from his father Yoshikazu.
333. *the client . . . entertain the gathering*: An important part of a monk's or a priest's work was to provide the Buddhist service for the various commemorations after the death of a family member, which were usually held at the house.
334. *Here is a strange . . . the monk Tōren*: The holy man of Watanabe is unidentified. Watanabe was in present-day Osaka. Plume grass (*susuki*) was an important poetic trope, so such arcane details would have been of great interest to poets such as Tōren (dates unknown).
335. *'Swiftness will always bear fruit'*: From *Analects* XVII, 6.
336. *'He'll be so besotted . . . his own personal buddha'*: The translation here follows Shōtetsu-bon.
337. *such judgements cannot be applied . . . to Buddhist teachings*: The various teachings found among the sects and sutras may differ, but they should not therefore be dismissed as wrong, since all point to the same truth.
338. *the Koga–Nawate road*: On the south-west outskirts of the capital.
339. *Jizō*: Guardian deity of children and travellers.
340. *Palace Minister Koga*: Minamoto no Michimoto (1240–1308).
341. *commander*: One of the Right and Left commanding officers of the Palace Guards. Michimoto was Commander of the Right from 1278 to 1288.
342. *the sacred palanquin . . . the Wakamiya Shrine in Tōji*: The protective deity of Tōji Temple in Nara (Kenkō in fact mistakes the temple) had been ensconced in a shrine in the grounds of the capital's Tōdaiji Temple. It was now being returned in state to its former home.
343. *The Minamoto nobles*: The deity belonged to Iwashimizu Hachiman Shrine, an important shrine to the south of the capital whose deity was worshipped by the powerful Minamoto clan, to which Michimoto belonged.
344. *the Tsuchimikado Minister of State*: Minamoto no Sadazane (1241–1306).
345. *the Hokuzanshō . . . the Saikyūki*: The *Hokuzanshō* (1012–20) is a collection detailing old customs and rites, compiled by Fujiwara Kintō (966–1041). The *Saikyūki* is a similar but earlier collection by Minamoto no Takakira (914–82).
346. *The term jōgaku . . . the Engishiki*: *Jōgaku* (fixed quota) generally applied to the number of monks in a temple. The *Engishiki*

was an important fifty-volume compendium of ceremonial regulations and customs compiled in 927.

347. *Seiji Yōryaku*: A 130-volume compendium of laws and court regulations produced around 1006. Here and in the previous section, Kenkō is documenting ancient precedent rather than present fact, probably in reference to a current debate on the question.

348. *Abbot Gyōsen of Yokawa*: Nothing is known of Gyōsen. Yokawa was one of the three main temple complexes of the great Enryakuji Temple on Mount Hiei, to the north-east of the capital.

349. *no ritsu mode*: The Chinese *ryo*, a seven-note scale built on G, is associated with a more coolly 'rational' style than the more 'emotional' Japanese *ritsu*, built on D.

350. *the Jijūden*: A building in the middle of the Inner Palace grounds.

351. *Taibon and Gejō*: The two stupas said to have been erected by the pious King Bimbisāra along the road to Vulture Peak travelled by those who came to hear the Buddha's sermon.

352. *all the gods gather at the Grand Shrine in Ise*: It was believed that in the tenth month all the gods of Japan go to the Sun Goddess Amaterasu's Grand Shrine at Ise, and are thus absent from their own shrines.

353. *associated with inauspicious events*: Early death, earthquakes, etc. were noted to have followed various past imperial pilgrimages made in the tenth month.

354. *Tenjin Shrine . . . Kurama Temple*: Tenjin Shrine on Gojō Street in the south of the capital was particularly associated with salvation from plague, as was Yuki (or Yugi) Shrine, at the entrance to the temple complex on Mount Kurama north of the capital.

355. *Abbot Jie . . . the Invocation and Vows to the Founder*: A document written as a prayer to the founder of the Tendai Sect, Saichō (767–822), making a vow in return for the answer to the prayer. Jie, or Ryōgen (912–85), was the eighteenth abbot of Enryakuji Temple on Mount Hiei.

356. *water and fire . . . although containers are*: When a household suffered some inauspicious event, the water and fire of that house were also considered to be polluted. The relevance of this to the previous discussion is unclear.

357. *the now-deceased Tokudaiji Minister of the Right*: Probably refers to Fujiwara Kintaka (see note 60 above).

358. *his central gate*: The room-width covered bridgeway connecting two buildings at his residence.

359. *the Minister*: Fujiwara Sanemoto (1201–73).

360. *the Kameyama Residence*: See note 108.
361. *This Minister*: I.e. Sanemoto, as note 359 above.
362. *Abbot Kōshun of Kegon-in Temple*: Dates unknown. He was abbot of Tōji Temple from 1320 to 1323. Kegon-in was a subtemple in the Ninnaji Temple complex.
363. *the yobukodori*: An unidentified bird, possibly a cuckoo, whose song is associated with spring in early poetry.
364. *One Shingon text . . . a soul-returning ceremony*: A ceremony intended to draw a wandering soul back into the body. The text has not been identified.
365. *ground thrush*: White's ground thrush (*Turdus dauma*). The name (*nue*) also applied to a bird of fable with a monkey's head, raccoon's body, snake's tail and tiger's feet.
366. *the Manyōshū chōka poem*: Poem 5, by Prince Ikusa (dates unknown), in the first volume of the *Manyōshū* (eighth century), the earliest anthology of Japanese poetry. The *chōka* is a long verse form of alternating five- and seven-syllable units.
367. *Even the exemplary Yan Hui met with misfortune*: Yan Hui (see note 230) died young and impoverished.
368. *Humans . . . in heaven and earth*: A quotation from *Shu jing* (*The Book of Documents*).
369. *When lighting the charcoal . . . to prevent the lit coal from falling*: Room heating was by means of charcoal burned in portable braziers of various kinds. A pile of charcoal in the brazier was lit by placing a lit coal on it, an action usually performed with metal chopsticks. Various taboos surrounded the use of fire in the imperial presence.
370. *Yahata Shrine*: Yahata Shrine is an alternative name for Iwashimizu Hachiman Shrine (see note 110).
371. *The name of the musical piece . . . written with different characters*: The title was usually written with characters meaning 'Longing for her husband'. The alternative meaning is derived by writing the same sounds with different characters, meaning 'Love for the Lotus Mansion'.
372. *Wang Jian of the Jin dynasty*: Wang Jian (452–89) was in fact born after the Jin period (265–419). He was a high official. The famous story of his love for his lotus pond led to his house being given the name 'Lotus Mansion', to which the alternative title of the musical piece refers.
373. *the Chinese land known to us as Kaikotsu*: Chinese Huhe, a realm in the far west of China.

374. *Taira no Nobutoki*: (1238–1323) Provincial governor and later advisor to the shōgun. He was also known for his poetry. Kenkō may have heard this story from him when he visited Kamakura in around 1318.
375. *the Saimyōji Novice*: Hōjō no Tokiyori (see note 329). He took the tonsure in 1256.
376. *Hachiman Shrine in Tsurugaoka*: A shrine in Kamakura, an important place of worship for the shogun.
377. *Ashikaga Sama Novice*: Ashikaga Yoshiuji (1189–1254). Powerfully connected through marriage, he took the tonsure in 1241.
378. *Abbot Ryūben*: (1206–83), head of the Tsurugaoka Hachiman Shrine.
379. *dyed Ashikaga cloth*: Cloth dyed in the Ashikaga district (present-day Ibaraki prefecture), home of the Ashikaga clan, to which the Ashikaga Sama Novice belonged.
380. *Horikawa Mansion*: The home of the aristocratic Horikawa family, where Kenkō served as a young man.
381. *the Shijō Counsellor*: Fujiwara no Takasuke (1292–1352) (identification uncertain).
382. *Tatsuaki*: Toyohara Tatsuaki (1291–1363), a renowned player of the *shō* (a kind of pan pipes).
383. *the transverse flute*: A seven-holed flute. The following discussion concerns the relationship of the notes produced by fingering each hole, and the scales built on each of the notes.
384. *the master being awed by one who comes after*: A reference to the *Analects*.
385. *Kagemochi*: Ōga Kagemochi (1292–1376), provincial governor and renowned player of the transverse flute.
386. *The shō*: The pan pipes consist of a series of pipes, one tuned to every note.
387. *the bugaku performed at Tennōji Temple*: The *bugaku*, traditional court music and dance, performed on ritual occasions by the musicians and dancers of Shitennōji, an ancient and important temple in present-day Osaka.
388. *Prince Shōtoku*: See note 15 above.
389. *the ōshiki mode*: A mode or scale roughly equivalent to the C minor scale of Western music.
390. *between the Nehan and the Shōryō ceremonies*: The Nehan ceremonies, on the fifteenth day, marked the Buddha's death, and the Shōryō ceremonies, on the twenty-second day, commemorated the death of Shōtoku Taishi.

391. *Mujō Hall of Gion Shōja*: Gion Shōja, or Jetavana Temple, was given to Sakyamuni Buddha by a disciple. The Anitya (Japanese *mujō*, impermanence) Hall in its north-west corner, the monks' hospital, was said to ring its bells when a monk died.
392. *Saionji Temple*: See section 50. It used to stand where Kinkakuji Temple (the Golden Pavillion) now stands in northern Kyoto.
393. *Jōkongō-in*: A temple in the Saga area north-west of the capital.
394. *fourth-rank constabulary scholars*: Men versed in the legal codes, who served in the law enforcement agencies.
395. *the Kenji and Kōan eras*: 1275–88.
396. *the constabulary guards in the festival procession*: The constabulary guards (*hōben*) were pardoned criminals employed by the police department, who acted as guards in the procession of the great Kamo festival in the fourth month. By tradition, their clothing was elaborately decorated for the occasion.
397. *suikan robe*: An abbreviated form of normal court attire.
398. *Jōganbō of Takedani . . . Tōnijō no In*: Jōganbō (Sōgen, 1168–1251) was a recluse monk who lived in the valley of Takedani to the south-west of the capital. He was a follower of Hōnen (1133–1212), who taught that salvation could be achieved by chanting *nenbutsu* (the name of Amida). Tōnijō no In (1232–1304) was a daughter of the high-ranking Saionji Saneuji and later empress.
399. *The Kōmyō Shingon and the Hōkyōin Darani*: The Kōmyō Shingon is a magic spell which extinguishes sin. The Hōkyōin Darani, also a magic spell, ensures rebirth in paradise for those in hell. Both are part of the rites of the esoteric Shingon Buddhist sect.
400. *The Tazu Minister's*: Kujō Motoie (1203–80). He was an accomplished poet.
401. *Arimune*: Abe Arimune (dates unknown).
402. *Ō no Hisasuke . . . the novice Michinori . . . Iso no Zenji*: Ō no Hisasuke (1212–95), a top musician of his day. Fujiwara no Michinori (1106–59), a famously learned courtier who took the tonsure in 1144. Iso no Zenji (dates unknown), a dancer whose fame rests on her being the mother of Shizu, the mistress of the great warrior Yoshitsune (see note 414 below).
403. *the shirabyōshi*: A style of song and dance extremely popular at the time; the dance was performed by women in men's costume, accompanied by flute and drums. The songs were often accounts of the deities of temples and shrines. The name also applied to the dancers.

404. *Minamoto no Mitsuyuki*: (1163–1244), a provincial governor and important scholar and poet.
405. *Kamegiku*: (Dates unknown), a *shirabyōshi* dancer who was a favourite of Gotoba.
406. *the days of Retired Emperor Gotoba*: This refers specifically to his time as retired emperor, 1198–1221.
407. *former provincial governor of Shinano called Yukinaga*: This probably refers to Nakayama Yukinaga (dates unknown), who was governor not of Shinano (present-day Nagano prefecture) but of Shimotsuke (present-day Ibaraki prefecture). This section provides the sole evidence for the attribution of Yukinaga as the author of *The Tale of the Heike* (early thirteenth century, depicting the struggles between the Heike and Minamoto clans).
408. *yuefu*: A ballad form frequently found in the poems of Bai Juyi.
409. *'Dance of the Seven Virtues'*: A poem in the *yuefu* form by Bai Juyi that alludes to the dance of that name traditionally performed at the court, which depicted the seven virtues of warfare.
410. *'Young Master Five Virtues'*: The title Young Master (*kanja*) was given to youths (Yukinari would have been in late middle age).
411. *Jichin*: (1155–1225), a renowned poet, more commonly known as Jien. He appears in section 67 as Abbot Yoshimizu.
412. *The Tale of the Heike . . . the blind reciter Shōbutsu*: Shōbutsu is a largely legendary figure known as the founder of the blind minstrel (*biwa hōshi*) tradition of sung recitations of *The Tale of the Heike*. This passage is the basis for the tradition that Yukinaga was its creator.
413. *This is why . . . Enryakuji*: Enryakuji, the great Tendai temple on Mount Hiei, north-east of the capital, was the temple to which Jichin and consequently Yukinaga were attached.
414. *Yoshitsune, the Kurō Lieutenant*: Minamoto no Yoshitsune (1159–89), who, with his brother Yoritomo (1147–99), was a key player in the Genpei Wars depicted in *The Tale of the Heike*. His official title was Kurō Lieutenant (Hōgan).
415. *Noriyori, or Kaba no Kanja*: Minamoto no Noriyori (?–1193), a younger brother of Yoshitsune and Yoritomo, who was dispatched to fight the Heike but subsequently executed on suspicion of treason. Kaba no Kanja was his official title.
416. *biwa reciters of the Tale*: Blind minstrels who recited the *Tale of the Heike* while accompanying themselves on the *biwa* (see note 38 above).
417. *The Six Hour Praises . . . Anraku, a disciple of the holy man Hōnen*: The Six Hour Praises (*rokuji raisan*) is a hymn in praise of the Bud-

dha's virtues, chanted at six fixed times throughout the day. Anraku (or Junsai, ?–1207), a preacher of Hōnen's Amidist faith, gained a strong following through his practice of devotions at fixed hours.

418. *an Uzumasa monk named Zenkanbō*: Zenkanbō is unidentified. Uzumasa was an area in the north-west of the capital, the site of Kōrakuji Temple, to which the monk may have belonged.

419. *the One Thought nenbutsu*: (*Ichinen no nenbutsu*), this probably refers to the belief among some of Hōnen's followers that a single recitation of the *nenbutsu* would result in rebirth in Amida's paradise.

420. *the time of Retired Emperor Gosaga*: He reigned 1242–6, although the reference may include his time as retired emperor.

421. *the Service Hymn*: (*Hōjisan*), a form of hymn interpolated into the recitation of the Amida Sutra.

422. *Senbon shaka nenbutsu . . . in the Bun'ei period*: The *shaka nenbutsu* was a ceremonial chant performed at Daihōonji Temple in the Senbon district of the capital, before an image of Sakyamuni's death and entry into Nirvana (see note 463 below). Nyorin Shōnin (Chōkū, dates unknown) was a high-ranking monk at Daihōonji. The Bun'ei period was from 1264 to 1275.

423. *Myōken's*: Unknown. Possibly an early sculptor of Buddhist images.

424. *The Gojō Palace*: A palace complex in the Gojō–Ōmiya area of the capital, occasionally used as an imperial residence.

425. *The Tō Grand Counsellor*: Nijō Tameyo (1250–1338), an important poet and Kenkō's teacher. The Gojō palace burned down when he was twenty-one.

426. *a fox*: Foxes were commonly believed to be shape-changers, able to assume human form.

427. *The Superintendant Novice Sono*: Probably Fujiwara Motouji (1211–82), who founded the Sono school of cuisine.

428. *the Kitayama Minister Novice*: Possibly Saionji Sanekane (1249–1322) (see note 218 above).

429. *The Histories*: The Chinese historical classics, such as *Records of the Historian* (Japanese *Shiki*, Chinese *Shiji*), an important early Chinese history compiled by Sima Qian (?145–86).

430. *an old wooden ladle whose handle could be used*: The use of a piece cut from the handle of a wooden ladle (*hishaku*) for fashioning a *biwa* bridge is mentioned in musicians' manuals, but is the kind of esoterica only musicians would know.

431. *there was no need for such finesse*: The blind *biwa* reciters were entertainers, of low status, and thus not worthy of such refinements.

432. *the kind of wood used for containers*: Cypress (*hinoki*) wood stripped into thin peels that are curved to form boxes.
433. *Tamba*: Tamba province spanned present-day Kyoto and Hyogo prefectures.
434. *the deity of the great Izumo Shrine has been installed*: Izumo Shrine, in present-day Shimane prefecture, is an ancient and important shrine dedicated to the god Ōkuninushi no mikoto. This subshrine near the capital was established to worship the same god.
435. *a certain Shida*: Unidentified.
436. *Shōkai*: Unidentified.
437. *guardian Chinese lion and Korean dog*: Stone images that traditionally guard the entrance to a shrine, one on either side, facing outward.
438. *a willow-work stand*: (*Yanaibako*, literally 'willow box'). Here it refers to a stand on low legs, made of triangular slats of willow wood.
439. *Sanjō Minister of the Right*: Unidentified.
440. *the Kadenokōji house*: Kadenokōji was a family line of the Fujiwaras that specialized in calligraphy.
441. *Chikatomo*: Nakahara Chikatomo (dates unknown). He was a bodyguard to Emperors Horikawa and Toba.
442. *Saishōkō-in*: A temple that stood in the south-east of the capital, in the vicinity of present-day Sanjūsangendō Temple.
443. *our present emperor*: Godaigo. He was a crown prince from 1308 to 1318.
444. *the Horikawa Grand Counsellor*: Probably Minamoto Tomochika (1294–?).
445. *the passage about Confucius hating to see purple trumping red*: 'I hate purple that replaces red' (*Analects XVII*, 18). This is taken to be a reference to a world in which the false or complex (the secondary colour purple) can trump the true and simple (the primary colour red).
446. *Lord Teika*: Fujiwara Teika (1162–1241), a renowned poet and scholar.
447. *the two words for sleeve,* sode *and* tamoto: *Sode* refers to the whole sleeve, while *tamoto* strictly refers to the pocket of the sleeve. Both appear frequently in traditional poetry as tropes for sorrow and parting.
448. *the old poem*: This poem, by Ariwara no Muneyana (?–898), is included in the great imperial anthology *Kokinshū*.
449. *Teika writes of this very pretentiously*: The source for this anecdote remains unknown.

450. *the Kujō Chief Minister Koremichi*: Fujiwara no Koremichi (1093–1165). It was the custom to submit a list of one's achievements in hopes of promotion.
451. *The inscription on the bell . . . Lord Arikane*: The temple bell was inscribed with a phrase in Chinese that reproduced the writing of a chosen calligrapher. Jōzaikō-in was a temple in the eastern foothills of the capital, already a ruin in Kenkō's day. Sugawara Arikane (1249–1321) was a scholar of Chinese literature and tutor to a succession of imperial princes.
452. *Lord Yukifusa*: Kadenokōji Yukifusa (?–1337), a renowned calligrapher.
453. *'Beyond the flowers . . . a hundred miles away'*: No source has been found for this quotation, which would have been in Chinese, although it is similar to words in a poem by Bai Juyi.
454. *composed in the Yangtang scheme*: A tonal rhyme scheme in Chinese verse. The discussion concerns the different tones of the words proposed.
455. *'a hundred miles' . . . should be 'some furlongs'*: The discussion of these various units of measurement (*ri*, *kō* and *ho*) hinges on matters of rhyme.
456. *'Some leagues' is indeed suspicious*: The words here in brackets may be Kenkō's own later comment, or a later interpolation by a copyist.
457. *Three Pagodas Pilgrimage*: A circuit of the three main pagodas (East, West and Yokawa) of the temple complex of Enryakuji on Mount Hiei.
458. *'Ryōge-in'*: One of the sub-temples of the Yokawa temple group.
459. *by Sari or Kōzei*: Two great calligraphers, Fujiwara Sari (944–98) and Fujiwara Kōzei (Yukinari) (972–1027).
460. *the holy priest Dōgen . . . the Eight Calamities*: For Dōgen and Naranda Temple, see note 318 above. The Eight Calamities of Buddhist doctrine are: sorrow, joy, suffering, pleasure, the urge to understand, the urge to distinguish, expiration and inspiration.
461. *beyond the screen*: Kenkō was listening as a lay person, so was separated from the monks.
462. *accompanied Abbot Kenjō to see the Perfumed Water Purification*: Kenjō (1280–1333) was head priest of Tōji Temple. The Perfumed Water Purification (*kaji kōzui*) was a Shingon ritual performed at Shingon-in, the purified water being later taken to the palace and applied to the emperor's body.
463. *On the fifteenth day of the second month . . . the Senbon Temple*: The day of the Buddha's entry into Nirvana, when ceremonies

were performed before a displayed depiction of the scene. The Senbon Temple is Daihōonji (see note 422 above).

464. *rōshuku days*: Chinese astronomy traditionally divided the constellations into twenty-eight *shuku* or houses, and related them to the calendrical days and months.

465. *'watchful eyes . . . snare him in the dark'*: A poetic passage weaving together elegant images commonly found in love poetry. The romantic ideal was of a young couple who must meet in secret because of family disapproval and prying eyes.

466. *'answer the call of any current'*: From a famous poem by Ono no Komachi (fl. *c*.833–57), composed in response to an invitation.

467. *'forging their way through the dense autumn woods'*: A common poetic trope for difficulties endured.

468. *'A buddha is what a human becomes'*: A rather simplified answer fitting a child's question. It is based on the idea that humans have an original buddha nature and can attain enlightenment, as did the historical Buddha.

Penguin Classics

THE ANALECTS
CONFUCIUS

'The Master said, "If a man sets his heart on benevolence, he will be free from evil" '

The Analects are a collection of Confucius' sayings brought together by his pupils shortly after his death in 497 BC. Together they express a philosophy, or a moral code, by which Confucius, one of the most humane thinkers of all time, believed everyone should live. Upholding the ideals of wisdom, self-knowledge, courage and love of one's fellow man, he argued that the pursuit of virtue should be every individual's supreme goal. And while following the Way, or the truth, might not result in immediate or material gain, Confucius showed that it could nevertheless bring its own powerful and lasting spiritual rewards.

This edition contains a detailed introduction exploring the concepts of the original work, a bibliography and glossary and appendices on Confucius himself, *The Analects* and the disciples who compiled them.

Translated with an introduction and notes by D. C. Lau

read more

PENGUIN CLASSICS

SANSHIRO
NATSUME SŌSEKI

'Even bigger than Japan is the inside of your head. Don't ever surrender yourself - not to Japan, not to anything'

Sōseki's work of gentle humour and doomed innocence depicts twenty-three-year-old Sanshiro, a recent graduate from a provincial college, as he begins university life in the big city of Tokyo. Baffled and excited by the traffic, the academics and - most of all - the women, Sanshiro must find his way amongst the sophisticates that fill his new life. An incisive social and cultural commentary, *Sanshiro* is also a subtle study of first love, tradition and modernization, and the idealism of youth against the cynicism of middle age.

In his introduction, Haruki Murakami reflects on his fascination with Sanshiro, how the story differs from a European coming-of-age novel and why it has come to be a perennial classic in Japan. This edition also contains suggestions for further reading, notes and a chronology.

Translated by Jay Rubin, with an introduction by Haruki Murakami

THE STORY OF PENGUIN CLASSICS

Before 1946 … 'Classics' are mainly the domain of academics and students; readable editions for everyone else are almost unheard of. This all changes when a little-known classicist, E. V. Rieu, presents Penguin founder Allen Lane with the translation of Homer's *Odyssey* that he has been working on in his spare time.

1946 Penguin Classics debuts with *The Odyssey*, which promptly sells three million copies. Suddenly, classics are no longer for the privileged few.

1950s Rieu, now series editor, turns to professional writers for the best modern, readable translations, including Dorothy L. Sayers's *Inferno* and Robert Graves's unexpurgated *Twelve Caesars*.

1960s The Classics are given the distinctive black covers that have remained a constant throughout the life of the series. Rieu retires in 1964, hailing the Penguin Classics list as 'the greatest educative force of the twentieth century.'

1970s A new generation of translators swells the Penguin Classics ranks, introducing readers of English to classics of world literature from more than twenty languages. The list grows to encompass more history, philosophy, science, religion and politics.

1980s The Penguin American Library launches with titles such as *Uncle Tom's Cabin*, and joins forces with Penguin Classics to provide the most comprehensive library of world literature available from any paperback publisher.

1990s The launch of Penguin Audiobooks brings the classics to a listening audience for the first time, and in 1999 the worldwide launch of the Penguin Classics website extends their reach to the global online community.

The 21st Century Penguin Classics are completely redesigned for the first time in nearly twenty years. This world-famous series now consists of more than 1300 titles, making the widest range of the best books ever written available to millions – and constantly redefining what makes a 'classic'.

The Odyssey continues …